OF LOVE

FROM HEAVENS ABOVE

MICKEY NIVELLI

ECHOES OF LOVE FROM HEAVENS ABOVE
Mickey Nivelli

Visit www.echoesoflove.com for more details and information
on Bulk Purchase Discounts.

First Paperback Edition: January 2003

ISBN: 0-9730189-0-9

Library of Congress Registration Number: TXu-1-017-032
Code: 1/B

National Library of Canada Cataloguing in Publication
    I. Title.
    PS3614.I94E24 2002   811'.6
    C2002-901870-6

Contents

Mickey with his Mentor

Dr. Harindranath Chattopadhyaya, lovingly referred to as "Dada", was one of the most popular and respected poets of India. Dr. Rabindranath Tagore, Nobel Prize winning writer and poet, fondly said of Dada, "My mantle now falls on Harin."

I learned a lot from Dada in almost three decades of my association with him. He could weave my ideas and thoughts into silken poetry for my movies: *"The Right and the Wrong"*, *"Caribbean Fox"*, *"Man from Africa"* and *"Girl from India"*. The depth, meaning and lyrics of his words laced my writings with new perspectives and dimensions.

Back in the late 1980's, when I first showed Dada the manuscript of Lotte's story, he strongly felt that this saga of eternal love must be expressed and enshrined in the timeless format of poetry. "Let me set your words into rhyme," he exuded. "It will be the crowning glory of my life." Dada was 90 years old then and I was reluctant to burden him with this task, due to his frail and failing health. But he was insistent, and I found it difficult to refuse.

Dada passed away on June 23, 1990.

He was my Guru, my inspiration and my strength. To honor his memory and his contribution to my life, I collected whatever work he had done on my manuscript and published it in India as a book entitled: *"The Power of Love"*. Many events have transpired since then, and many new chapters have been added to the saga. But Dada's voice has kept reverberating in my ears: "Complete Lotte's story in poetry because the spirit of both is eternal."

Dada was a genius. He could have completed the task swiftly and added that lustrous sheen, had he remained healthy and alive. It has taken me much longer and I received help from many to whom I will remain grateful. But, above all, I remain humbly grateful to my beloved Dada for his unrelenting faith in this project and for his undying inspiration from the eternal realms of heaven.

Mickey Nivelli
New York, 2002

On the Cusp of Eternity

Lotte had been unconscious for many a day.
With devoted vigil, we continued to pray.
Hans, her beloved for over twenty years
sighed, "She won't revive." We were in tears.

While she waded in the clouded twilight zone
her torments hung in limbo, or were bygone.
Of inherent human powers, Lotte is an example.
God's gift of resilience, we all have in ample.

Lotte triumphed by tapping into this repository
that had successfully shielded her from bigotry.
Her 88 tumultuous years became a beacon
illuminating the many battles she had won.

She channeled heaven's echoes of love
and with this power could rise above
the traumas of her torrid throes.
When we first met, *the moment froze!*
Truth became stranger when Lotte could,
for me, incarnate a mystical motherhood.
The divine dynamics of her visions vast,
forever connected my future with her past.

"Prepare for her funeral," Hans suddenly said,
"Lotte's time is waning . . . she'll soon be dead."
During her lifetime she had suffered stringent strife.
Hans loved her but scoffed her faith in afterlife.

Lotte focused on the grandeur of life beyond.
Hans, a traditionalist, would brusquely respond:
"I don't trust the unknown or the invisible."
(A prisoner of senses, the physically tangible).
She tried sincerely to make him understand.
He dismissed each attempt with a reprimand.

Deep insights can be discovered in abundance
in Lotte's tragedies and miraculous renaissance . . .
for she radiated the epitome of love to unveil
many facets of spirituality – the essence of her tale.

The Beginning

Souls are encased for a purpose absolute,
to begin life in a form that is pure and cute.
Each one, an extension of God's own nature
that He entrusts to us to love and nurture.

This impressionable entity absorbs all it hears,
we feed it our individual values and fears.
Environment does not forever pollute the pure
soul within the body, for its divinity is secure.

When Lotte was a baby, Edith, her older sister
would love to hug and tenderly kiss her.
In Witten – Germany – Edith, then two-years-old
ecstatically exclaimed, "She is a doll of gold."

She joyfully kissed her cheeks, forehead and toes,
followed by her fingers, ears and nose.
For Sybilla and Adolph their new born daughter
would fill their lives with love and laughter.

Edith's raptures knew no bound.
Bursting with joy she pranced around
chanting and singing, "A doll, a doll
has been sent to us, dainty and small.
She has rosy cheeks and beautiful eyes.
A gift from the heavens and the skies."

Neighbors asked Edith, "Will you some day
let us hold your doll to hug and play?
We promise not to hurt your doll!"
Little Edith replied, "Can I trust you all?"
Lotte bloomed and soon began sensing
several shades of love's toning and coloring.

Sybilla and Adolph sparkled with her light
and they loved their special baby day and night.
Neighbors visited, played games and would coo.
Lotte's horizons expanded and her love grew.

After gamboling with other children in the park
she would return with Edith, just before dark.
Like Mary's little lamb wherever Edith went,
Lotte followed her, bubbling with merriment.

Most of Witten came to know,
of cute little Lotte, always aglow!
Edith was sister and friend to this innocent sprite
who was flushed with colors of spring so bright.

Two ideal sisters, both verily
a picture of love, playing merrily.
They made cute little toys out of clay.
Then fought over them, in an innocent way.

Both girls grew up, year by year,
in this sweet affectionate atmosphere.
Edith, as Lotte's playmate and guide,
protected her from every side.

Lotte's father, Adolph Sommers (above) and Germany's Vice-chancellor,
Adolph Hitler, had the same first names but little else in common.
Adolph Sommers was a loving father and a paragon of virtues, whereas
Hitler was a hateful human whose crimes tainted civilization forever.

The Drums of War

Adolph Hitler and the Nazis sought
to derail destinies – or so they thought.
"Adolph is our beloved Fuhrer's first name,
any other is a mockery." A wild mob came.

They smashed Adolph Sommer's nameplate
in their blind rage and mindless hate.
"Adolph is the name of our great Hitler.
Change your name or be branded a traitor."

In their fanatic fury they ranted and fumed.
With venomous hatred they hysterically boomed,
"God, in His great wisdom, we Germans hear
speaking through our Fuhrer – Adolph Hitler.
German glory is synonymous with his name.
Dispel your name *Adolph* – or else do not blame
us for the consequences you will face . . .
your family's destruction and utter disgrace."

Adolph Hitler versus Adolph Sommer!
Who shall be the loser and who the winner?
In realms eternal, who will triumph later . . .
Lotte's loving father or the crazed dictator?

Adolph Sommer Succumbs to Stress

"Stay in a sanatorium. You need some rest,"
the doctor advised Adolph to what was best.
"I'll take Lotte . . . Edith, I think you had better
stay at home and help your mother."

A place for Lotte had been set apart
in the loving chambers of her father's heart.
Lotte loved her father very much . . .
his wisdom, values and paternal touch.

In the sanatorium Lotte had met
the doctor's daughter who, as yet,
spun youthful dreams without any end.
She shared them with her newfound friend.

They started sharing secrets very feminine.
Teenaged girls can often cross the line!
They played and chatted all day long.
Their time would flow like a sweet song.

Profiles of Love

"What kind of man do you wish to meet?"
"Understanding, sensitive and very sweet.
My dreams, Lotte, are defined and done.
Can all these qualities be found in one?

He must be handsome, pink in health,
and yes, it helps if he is blessed with wealth.
My man must have a true lover's heart . . .
his romantic overtures should be an art.

To win my heart I would love to see
him kneel when he proposes to me.
Then plant on my lips a romantic kiss,
pulsating with passion and celestial bliss."

"When I find him," Lotte began to enquire,
"how will I know it is he who I desire?"
"Don't you know that it has been said
that bells begin tinkling inside your head.
Any person struck by love knows
that the heart blossoms like a rose."

Lotte was rueful. She still had not met
a man of her desires – not just as yet.
Lotte and Edith had also shared some stages
of complexities involved during innocent ages.
They had both known many boys as friends,
with no designs to reach romantic ends.

Their parents taught them they must belong to those who believe and consider it wrong to be physically intimate . . . and not begin relationships that can steer them to sin.

Trauma of Father's Death

Adolph Sommer died due to a batch of insulin
that was contaminated. He died within
a short while after he was admitted.
The doctors in Witten were outwitted.

The fatally flawed insulin they had received,
was immediately dumped. The doctors heaved
a sigh of relief. Adolph's death was the price
that saved many lives. It was a sad sacrifice.

Lotte hysterically sobbed and cried,
when her beloved father died.
Edith's sorrow, however, remained unexpressed.
It lay bottled up, hidden deep in her breast.

Silent sorrows that she had deep down kept
disoriented Edith. She thought her father slept.
"Hush! Don't make any sounds," she said,
"you'll wake up Dad. He is not really dead."

At their black dresses, the sisters gazed
and realized Dad had died. They were dazed.
Curiously, they began laughing out loud.
Were they mocking their father's shroud?

During traumatic moments, peculiar behavior
often occurs but serves as a savior
that helps escape reality. A dose of laughter
soothes the pain, until truth dawns after.

Designed diversions help let loose
unbearable agony, like a gushing sluice.
It is a necessary device to mitigate grief.
The stricken grab whatever lends them relief.

Their father's death caused a cruel disruption,
because uncle started siphoning in his direction
the assets of the business. With deceits and hoax,
opportunists pounce to plunder vulnerable folks.

Uncle's shoddy treatment of their mother
multiplied their sorrows after the loss of father.
Sybilla was shattered. She needed tender care.
Her daughters nursed her. She had a lot to bear.

Like little mothers, they even fed her.
Widowhood crushes women. The feeble falter
through life's lonely paths. Relatives have beguiled
many a widow who faces life's turn of tide.

Even though Sybilla was heavy-hearted,
concerns for her children's welfare she imparted.
In life's adversities she clearly felt and saw,
an urgent need to find two sons-in-law.

"Hurry up daughters. Make your decisions.
Your husbands could support us in our missions.
While your father was alive, your uncle was meek.
Now look how he treats us. He has some cheek!"

Enter, a Swaggering Lover

A successful jewelry merchant, Larry Tower,
exuded an enticing and alluring power.
Edith got hooked and was a frequent visitor
at the shop of this charming Belgian jeweler.

Was it to negotiate bangles and rings,
or necklaces, chains and other precious things?
What secret yearnings made Edith wander
to Larry Tower's shop? Hmm . . . we wonder!

She would enter and cast a gracious glance.
Her demeanor obviously hinted at romance.
Was it a natural desire or was she frantic?
Tower responded and was being romantic.

Lotte was ecstatic and could not separate
romance from marriage in Edith's fate.
Was Edith merely another jewel
of Larry's collections? That would be cruel.

Larry was no stranger to the art of romancing.
He took Edith out for dinners and dancing.
After these outings, when Edith returned,
her body glowed, blushed and burned.

She floated on a cloud of an enchanting dream.
Larry loved Edith – or so it would seem.
Larry also greeted Lotte, oft and on.
She had no inkling he was a Don Juan.

Lotte was happy that Edith found her man.
Larry seemed genuine, his honor spic and span.
He was so very handsome and always well dressed
that even Sybilla Sommers was greatly impressed.

Edith announced to her mother, "I shall marry
no one else . . . not anyone – but Larry!"
Were this romantic couple secretly engaged?
Their marital plans seemed obviously staged.

For their early marriage, Lotte fervently prayed.
"Edith's happiness should not be delayed."
She hoped that Larry would faithfully hold
her sister's love, above his jewels and gold.

Lotte too found love. Since very long
she had loved music and classical song.
Her devotion to music would fully cover
all of her heart, like a passionate lover.

The songs she sang, each one a star,
portrayed love's reach to paradise afar.
Love and art helped make her realize
life's divine dimensions – a precious prize.

Her devotion and dedication were so sublime,
that her spirits would transcend space and time.
One day when her focus was very strong,
a familiar voice sliced into her song.

The intrusive element, Lotte saw,
was Larry her future brother-in-law.
"Lotte, please come with me down the road,
I need your help to write a love ode."

Maybe he wanted to formerly propose,
or seek another woman's advice . . . who knows?
In haste and anticipation, Lotte ran down.
Larry drove her to the outskirts of town.

He kept on driving. It was a long ride.
Then he parked, came close and tried
to deceptively entice her, "Lotte, I hope
you won't feel that I am a love-struck dope."

Something seemed wrong, Lotte was worried.
Larry changed his tone...his speech was hurried:
"Please understand Lotte, I cannot deny
that I love you. Let me explain why . . .

I did love your sister very much.
But one day when I felt the magic touch
of your hands, I was sensually stirred.
An attraction for you instantly occurred.

This obsession for you has struck me blind.
Please help me Lotte. I hope you don't mind."
Then he leaned forward and tried to plant a kiss.
"I truly love you . . . .don't take this amiss.
One destined and very happy day,
we will be married. What do you say?"

Lotte slapped him hard. "Leave me alone.
Dirty Larry . . . just take me home!"
The rebukes that followed, sharp as a knife,
Lotte hoped he'd remember all his life.

"You are vulgar and depraved.
My sister trusted you. She must be saved.
I see you are unworthy of her trust.
Scoundrel, go rub your nose in dust!
My revulsion for you is now absolute.
Now drive me back, you lecherous brute."

Exit, the Chastized Knave

Larry slinked away, never to come again.
Except once – but even that was all in vain.
By Larry's infidelity, Edith was dismayed.
Women are traumatized when they are betrayed.

They are fragile and are prone to trust -
traits that are beatific and august.
As Edith's sorrow and depression deepened,
Lotte watched her wilt and was saddened.
She became Edith's support and power.
A pillar of strength against Larry Tower.

It pained Lotte to see Edith dejected.
She realized her sister must be protected.
Lotte assumed the mantle of a little mother.
Past memories rolled by one after the other.

Down Memory Lane

The clock ticked back. The years turned over
to their golden days of a youthful summer.
"Our parents had taken us to a farm,
full of nature's wonderment and charm.
We saw a sight that lingers yet . . .
an incident Edith and I could never forget.

A grey hen calmly sauntered on the field,
leading her chicks and seeking some feed.
A dog sneaked up and began to stalk . . .
priming himself to attack her flock.

The hen fluffed her feathers, clawed and huffed,
with a mother's instincts her body was puffed.
To battle the dog, she swelled with defiance.
Was it maternal might or a crazed self-reliance?

For her chicks she was prepared to wage
a doomed battle, as we could gauge.
Bravado or strength? Be it understood,
God empowers the instincts of motherhood.

Even though the odds in battle are unequal,
mothers fight ferociously despite a sad sequel.
For the love of their offspring they gladly give
their very all . . . uncaring, if they perish or live.

Godhood and motherhood epitomize selflessness.
Yet both often suffer their children's selfishness.
The hen was a heroine. So without delay,
I grabbed a stick and chased the dog away."

Lotte's love had sprouted protective wings
to shield her sister from love's bitter stings.
Time healed Edith's pain. She did recover.
God helps good women find the right lover.

Like butterflies, love takes flight when pursued
but flutters back to you when sensitively wooed.
Edith was withdrawn, but her feminine vulnerability
charmed Hugo Weinberg and touched his sensibility.

Sybilla and Lotte saw Edith again gleam.
Husband and happy home were her dream.
After marrying Hugo, she could not stay.
To her husband's home, she was whisked away.

Finding True Love

One day Lotte visited a friend's home.
Her heart thenceforth ceased to roam.
On that auspicious day, she met a man -
Felix Joseph . . . was this a divine plan?

Her feelings for Felix made her start
to hear the sweet bells ring in her heart.
Something made her glow beneath her skin.
A wash of warmth meant love had crept in.

She felt intoxicated . . . heady with the wine
from Cupid's own cup, sparkling and divine.
A surreal lighthouse shone like never before
casting a radiant beam on her life's lonely shore.

They were destined to meet, Lotte was sure.
Felix had qualities, remarkable and pure.
Handsome and with a fabulous physical form,
his sense of calm could withstand any storm.
Later some friends told Lotte how
Felix also fell for her and made a vow . . .

"That glow in her eyes, so gypsy green,
predicts to me that she'll be my queen
and shall be mine in this life and afterlife.
We'll bond forever as husband and wife."

To mean so much, Lotte was flattered.
The attraction was mutual and so it mattered.
As a woman of her times, Lotte restrained
from displaying her feelings. Modesty prevailed.

She wished to maintain her feminine mystique
or risk being labeled easy and weak.
Physical intimacies are better enjoyed
after emotions blossom or there is a void.

Bonding in Love

Lust without love needs the propellers
of alcohol, drugs and whatever else conjures
superficial excitements – but the spiritual differs.
It is compassion over passion, a true lover prefers.

Lotte and Felix found their roseate paradise.
The love that glimmered from their eyes
was emotional and had a spiritual base.
Such bonds are blessed by an ethereal grace.

These commitments are eternal, rising far above
the lust and passions that masquerade as love.
Love is an unconditional, selfless experience.
It enriches the soul with divine deliverance.

Sublime sensitivities that transcend the flesh
embrace eternity to keep love forever fresh.
Lotte and Felix decided to control and restrain
physical passions to cultivate spiritual gain.

They liked each other, so without any fuss,
their wedding plans the families began to discuss.
Lotte was excited because now her life
was about to be fulfilled as Felix's wife.

The day that Lotte and Felix were wed,
everyone was excited and they had
gifts from friends, family, neighbors and
something they both did not understand . . .

Most gifts were for a baby – bottles and bibs,
soft woolen caps and two little cribs.
A child's stroller that hummed and talked.
Rattlers, balloons and toy bears that walked.

Were they expected to procreate so very soon?
That's a lot of pressure to put on a honeymoon.
Both mothers-in-law thought this good -
for couples bond better in parenthood.

A father's love for the child a mother bears
adds strength to the love that the couple shares.
Parenting can bestow upon a man
glories as great as those of a woman.

A mother and father's nurture must be equal
to beget for the child a bright sequel.
Parents and the environment mould and define
a child's character that is inherently divine.

Evil Looms Large

Diabolic events engulfed Germany.
Hitler was named Chancellor in 1933.
Jewish people, in each household far and near,
were terrorized by his thugs in S.S. gear.

The planned destruction was callous-hearted.
The mobs were frenzied. Kristallnacht started.
Nazi party leaders and their cadres incited
Germany's era of horrors. History was blighted.

Dark clouds began to overcast the skies.
Yet optimists assumed that people would realize
Hitler's demagogy. Germany had great physicians,
poets, scientists, philosophers and musicians.

In a splendid country a devilish head
would be crushed. No one did initially dread
the rabble-rousing Hitler's hypnotic spell.
How can skilful oratory unleash such hell?

Honeymoon in Paris

A honeymoon is often the first great chance
for physical passion, beyond virginal romance.
To tone excessive excitements, as is often done,
Felix began drinking to relax and loosen.

In most first times, expectations and fears
are often the cause of physical failures.
To overcome anxieties couples drink to bolster
fevered passions but end up with a hangover.

Felix felt misty in his intoxication for her.
Was it the awe of nudity first timers suffer?
Like many honeymooners, they were not fated
to consummate intimacies that they had initiated.

Men, more than women, during passionate excitement
are prone to suffer a physical impediment.
Felix and Lotte hoped this phase would pass,
by walking bare-footed on lush, cool grass.

They learnt the lessons that fleeting lust
is not as important as compassion and trust.
Couples bond better with sublime spiritual love . . .
the discovery of this is a divine treasure-trove.

Casual carnal encounters do not define
love eternal. Spiritual bonds are divine.
After bonding spiritually, their bodies would play
a physical and celestial symphony every day.

The Prophecy

During their honeymoon they chanced to meet
a fortune-telling Gypsy on a Paris street.
With colored ribbons adorning her head
she looked like an exotic flowerbed.

She wore colorful and loose hanging sleeves
embroidered with flowers and bright yellow leaves.
She wore a bulging stripe-lined skirt,
each stripe with other stripes seemed to flirt.

The dust in her travel-weary gypsy shoes
bespoke many a tale with myriad views.
She gazed at them with an enigmatic smile.
Her piercing eyes gleamed with gypsy guile.

With curiosity aroused they stopped by to
observe the Gypsy. "For the both of you
I have valuable predictions – which for a fee,
can be revealed. Your future I can clearly foresee.
Time shall confirm it all as I look,
and peer deep into both your lives' book.
Turbulent crisis can be seen by my eyes.
Trust me . . . for I am gypsy-wise."

They were not impressed. Her long painted nails
flickered on her fingers flaunting fairy tales.
"I can foretell your future," she pleaded.
They agreed on a fee that she needed.

"Your bodies first failed you in the quest for passion.
But these inhibitions were overcome in some fashion."
Her commonsense deductions were no prophecy.
The gypsy was cheating! Must they still pay her fee?

Then she looked at Lotte, like no other.
"To a son you shall be a most unique mother."
Again, a statement applicable to most women.
No prediction . . . something obvious and common.

"But how can you predict it will be a son?"
"I am a gypsy woman, I have done
forecasts for many. My psychic powers ensnare
the secrets of everyone, anywhere."

For most women the ultimate fulfillment
is motherhood, whether perceived or latent.
The Gypsy thus failed in the tests of foretelling.
But Felix had a question, his hopes were swelling.

"How soon to a son shall my Lotte give birth
and make me the proudest man on earth?"
The Gypsy addressed Felix: "Sad, but true,
the son she mothers, shall never see you."
Felix was angry. "Your prophecy I shall defy,
by singing for the baby his first lullaby."

After paying the lady, Felix and Lotte spent
some time around her steeped in argument.
They ignored her presence for a while.
The Gypsy drew Lotte's attention with a smile.

"The stars whisper in my gypsy ears
sadness and pain, for many long years.
But you will have forty years of married life."
Felix was ecstatic, "Forty years as my wife.
I want more, Gypsy fair and young,
far more years than I hear by your tongue."

Felix was not content with only forty years.
Were his hopes floating in a flood of tears
flowing down the cheeks of time? How could he know
about the unfolding destiny and impending sorrow?
But a son's prediction helped to bring
great happiness for him . . . he felt like a King.

Troubles Begin Brewing

Germans preferred peaceful progressive roads.
That changed dramatically by the Nazi goads.
Political poison began permeating the air.
The German gentility was laid threadbare.

Tragically, this great country became
synonymous with gas chambers and flame.
Contrary to its flourishing culture and flair,
diabolical decadence descended everywhere.

Hijacked by fascists, with foul and fiery breath,
it was transformed into an arena of death.
Hitler was a malicious, merciless monster.
If he was not in politics, he'd be a gangster.

His hypnotic spell made Germans choose
to torture humanity and do worse to Jews.
Many generations of Jews had been born
in Germany, where their allegiance was sworn.

Miffed Mothers-in-Law

Mothers-in-law for reasons rather curious
are rightly or wrongly dubbed notorious.
Disgruntled daughters-in-law often discuss:
"Look what these women have done to us."

"Mine is more dangerous than bombs and guns."
"They are jealous because we married their sons."
Another wife asked her husband (to test
his bias seriously, or perhaps in jest)
"Who do you love more? I need to see
if your mother is more important than me.
If you were only able to save one life from the sea,
who would you save . . . your mother or me?"

"An unfair question," the husband said.
"Not really. Who would you want dead?"
The husband offered a smart reply:
"I cannot swim, so how can I comply?"

"My mother-in-law wields so much power,
she makes me cringe, quiver and cower."
"Mine has a look that seems to thirst
with wanton hate. Her eyes bulge and burst."
"My old hag is jealous. Afraid of the truth
of having lost the green years of her youth."

"When mine is around I can not express fully
the love for my husband, leery of her jealousy."
"Since mine is old and I am young,
she has cultivated a cactus tongue."

"Mine is a cockatoo who always shrieks,
and prattles foolishly whenever she speaks."
"Mine is like a bull with pointed horns
her harsh abuses pierce like thorns."

"And what is mine? To say the least,
she is crazier than the wildest beast."
"In deep tragedy I am embedded.
I often regret ever having wedded."

"We have all told our problems, but Lotte now
it is your turn – give us your story, tell us how
you are being treated by your husband's mother?
How do you two get along with each other?"

Loving Mother-in-Law

Rosa was a special mother-in-law.
Her positive visions clearly saw
the wisdom of how happy her son would be,
if Lotte was loved as a part of the family.

She sought a daughter in her daughter-in-law.
So her love was without any blemish or flaw.
Kind feelings blossomed. Rosa was unique,
and Gustav, her husband, was loving and meek.

As Lotte's father-in-law, he was extremely good.
He was pious and worked hard for his livelihood.
Rosa also pitched in and contributed some more.
In her spare time she ran a millinery store.

She made great hats . . . an occasional good gown.
Rosa offered bargains to the whole town.
Her hats were special. The best that were there.
She could make hats to match every tint of hair.

Their neighborhood bubbled with friendly folk.
With warmth and affection, they lived and spoke.
Of all her four sons, Lotte's mindset
considered Felix to be the handsomest.

Their family's ancestors made their decision
to escape from Spain's infamous Inquisition.
They were forced to flee and migrate to Germany.
Their many generations adopted this great country.

They were loyal German citizens every bit.
It was their home and they loved it!
But what Hitler planned, with his insane obsession,
exceeded the sins of the Spanish Inquisition.

Felix's Foreboding

Felix was both intuitive and wise.
He was quick to calculate and surmise
that all five must start re-arranging
their lives because Germany was changing.

The Nazis desired a Germany rid of Jews.
The German-Jews were targeted to lose
all rights and status and exist as strangers
in their own homeland. Doom and dangers!

To oppressive new laws they were forced to bow.
The Nazi regime would not even allow
Jewish teachers to continue teaching.
Preachers had to refrain from preaching.

Jewish performers were also issued a warning . . .
they no longer had rights to be performing.
Lotte's uncle's visions were narrow and lacking
realistic perceptions – their life began cracking.

In their own country they felt estranged.
They could not cope. So much had changed.
Intellectuals and artists who felt insecure
fled elsewhere to escape this furor.

Creative energy suffocates and chokes.
It cannot flourish in a place that provokes
chaos and discrimination in the drive.
The able ones fled away to survive.

Antidote to Hate

Lotte and Felix's love began to flower
into being their source of strength and power.
This intangible wealth they cultivated was worth
much more than all the riches on earth.
Love helps people find the sacred line
that borders betwixt the human and divine.

As children of God, both Felix and Lotte,
knew their love would flourish through eternity.
Dark and evil forces may succeed for some time
to subdue those who are meek and sublime.

For short-term gains selfish people can
distort doctrines to help their unholy plan.
The success thus achieved and every gain
shall ultimately fragment and perish in vain.

A thousand year Nazi Reich . . . or even a million,
what value would it have in the eternal dominion?
How wise is it then to smear one's soul
in the pursuit of an inhuman, senseless goal?

Whoever misleads by bragging of superior birth,
is dishonoring God's power. For all those on earth
were created by Him and each one is His pride.
A masterpiece and miracle we dare not deride.

The arrogant few who nefariously try
to denigrate God by making people die,
incur His wrath in proportion, though late.
Divine justice prevails to damn their fate.

It may patiently shadow, loom and lurk
allowing rascals to repent. Then begins its work
of teaching thugs that the gift of might,
misused or abused, shall be their blight.

Oblivious to Eternal Laws, the Nazi serpent flared.
Intoxicated with power these crazed few dared
to wreak havoc and terror on humanity.
Could God ever forgive or show sympathy?

Dark deeds avoid wisdom's light.
Like thieves, they choose the darkness of night.
Democracy deters oppression and abuse.
In a dictator's regime evil smolders and brews.

Sense of Self-Preservation

For America the five made plans to leave
Sybilla, Edith, Lotte, Hugo and Felix did grieve
to leave their homeland. They were in tears.
It was here they were born and lived for years.

As German citizens (generation after generation),
they revered the country, felt a high veneration.
They prayed that Nazism was but a formal
fleeting phase and soon all would be normal.

But matters slid from bad to worse.
Germany reeked with the Nazi curse.
This family expedited their plans for traveling.
Their lives were at risk and unraveling.

To obtain American visas, they soon found
was possible only if finances were sound.
Felix requested a cousin in Amsterdam
to rent them a bank-box, as part of their plan.

Beyond the Nazi reach, their secure bank-box
could hide enough money, jewelry and stocks.
Felix traveled to Holland regularly to arrange
the purchase of diamonds from the stock exchange.

Each new addition to whatever they had
brought them closer to their goal. They were glad!
When they saved enough, they could relax and smile.
But this made their uncle contrary and hostile.

Edith meticulously carted crates to the ship.
All in secrecy, lest the authorities thwart their trip.
They started dreaming of life in a democracy
where all people live as equals and free.

The fervent five who had saved, thanked
God when the required amount had been banked.
American visas could now be sought
to escape this megalomaniac despot.

Sybilla was happy to remain together
with all her children who assured her:
"Mother, we shall never leave you alone.
Your love is our life's cornerstone."

Horrible human atrocities however intense,
are overcome by love's bonding essence.
Without their mother the four could have easily gone,
but the five had a bond . . . she should never be left alone.

Family Betrayal gets Felix Arrested

The Nazis arrested Felix and then set a fat fee
to release him – an exorbitant levy for his liberty.
To retrieve him Lotte would pay any price.
Her own life too she would gladly sacrifice.

"Don't leave this country. We will protect
you and other useful citizens we select.
Help us fulfill Hitler's dreams, then you will see
how well you are treated and maybe set free.
We treat our friends like a protected lot
but you must surrender all you have got."

Those were Nazi promises written on water
to lure the trusting, but these five were smarter.
They did not disclose what was lying in their box
in Amsterdam, stashed away and safely locked
by their trustworthy cousin. They were comforted,
for their assets they knew were well protected.

A Shocking Discovery

Then came the greatest of all their shocks.
The cousin had usurped everything in the box.
He did what even the most criminal cad
would hesitate to do. They were raving mad.

"Why, dear cousin? We had trusted you!"
"This trust helped me do what I could do.
Is this not done by many a trustee?
Who has more priority? You or me?"

Cheated and doomed by this devious theft,
the fate of the five was dismal and bereft.
Their cousin who had so mercilessly spent,
what was their lifeline, did not even repent.

The Toll of Time

The 9th of November, 1938,
dramatically changed the Jewish fate.
Fiendish mobs, fuelled by fevered heat,
incited violence in every German street.

Targeting Jewish homes and commercial property
for attack they unleashed, what all feared to be,
the end of all humane traits that keep evil at bay.
A glimpse of the pending doomsday.

Stores and wayside booths were set on fire.
Diabolic destruction ruled this quagmire.
Upholstered furniture, drapes, sofas and beds,
were yanked down and wantonly ripped to shreds.

Costly porcelains, curios and figurines,
with works of art were smashed to smithereens.
The mob hysteria and its violent thirst
for destruction, depicted men at their worst.

Their ferocious frenzy made every room
of Jewish homes feel like a tomb.
Grim death pirouetted on its ballerina toes.
Grand pianos, artifacts, paintings and radios,
lay fragmented on streets, now rotting stuff.
Yet, for the Nazis, this was not enough.

From their homes the Jews were driven out.
Many skulls were broken with clout upon clout.
The wounded young ran blood-painted.
The old panicked or in fear, just fainted.

Felix and Hugo during this disruption of order
were, by chance, near the Holland border.
The women hoped that they both would go
away, lest they be arrested by the Gestapo.

Both the husbands could have easily fled.
But did not – fearing their families would be dead.
Love for their wives froze them in their track.
For Lotte and Edith, Felix and Hugo turned back.

"You should have escaped," Mother cried in anguish.
"Now all five of us shall together languish."
Felix and Hugo were immediately arrested.
The American dreams of all five were truncated.

The three women who were now left behind
were subjected to treatment most unkind.
They were trampled and beaten with a stick.
Sybilla, being older, became very sick.

They were then trotted off to a police station.
Treated as aliens, in their own birth nation.
"We can return your husbands to end your sorrow,
if you bring us more money by the morrow."

With so much lost, they were left with nothing.
Broke and helpless, they could not pay anything.
They pleaded for loans from people they knew.
But these were horrible times to be a Jew.

Farewell Letter from Felix's Parents

Dear Felix and Lotte, they're taking us away.
Where to or why, nobody can say.
Tomorrow we depart and so children tonight
to you, our most beloved, we hereby write.

As we write, the tears flow from our eyes.
This tragedy cuts deeper than we realize.
They took our all. It was banditry beyond belief.
No one offered us consolation or relief.

We hope the horrible grief that is ours
does not plague you. The Nazi powers
are inflicting upon us unthinkable crimes.
May God be with you during these times.

Maintain your faith, don't let an evil clown
with delusions of Godhood, pull you down.
God breathes life into babes in wombs.
The devil's disciples dispatch them to tombs.

Dear children, don't hate even those who,
in the grips of insanity, are despising you.
Two wrongs do not ever make a right.
Let villains be blighted. You remain upright.

We are helpless against this sad separation
being caused by our unexpected incarceration.
Without seeing you we have to sadly depart.
Our pain is acute . . . it wrenches our heart.

If we don't ever meet in our physical bodies,
we shall be waiting for you wherever God is.
By His amazing grace we'll all meet again.
The bonds of love will forever sustain.

Your mother, my beloved daughter Lotte,
needs you and Felix so you both must see
she is never left alone. These times are fraught
with an evil that defies sane human thought.

Good-bye beloved children. We shall not die in vain.
Our physical losses shall become a spiritual gain.
This is what matters in our divine domain.
As eternal beings we shall all meet again.

The Uprooted Five

The five were by the Gestapo shifted
to Cologne, where they now drifted
like waves in the sea. They were not knowing
to where, how or why they were going.

With other captured families they had to share
putrid spaces. Felix and Hugo were made to bear
hard labor like slaves. The Nazi lust
made them toil in conditions most unjust.

Choking with coal-dust, a blackened Felix came
very late one day, stooping low with shame.
His captors, to ridicule him, had kept piling
task upon task until his strength began failing.

His parents' disappearance created a deep void.
It did not fill, however hard they tried.
To soothe the loss of his father and mother
Lotte and Felix would embrace each other.

In Felix, she saw glimmers of her brother, Erich,
whose sudden death in his crib was a tragedy which
often occurs. All new mothers could prevent
such accidents, if their vigil does not relent.

Soon after each sister's marriage had begun,
both Edith and Lotte had wished for a son.
Were the sisters unconsciously seeking their brother?
If you lose a loved one you try to find another.

Tearing Loved-ones Apart

"All men of this household, Jew by Jew,
tomorrow morning at eight, must join the queue.
Hugo Wienberg and Felix Joseph must, unescorted,
join the lines of all men being transported."

Edith was worn out and despite being weak,
shocked everyone by slapping the man's cheek.
"You can't take our men." Edith declared.
Seething at her gall, the Nazi glared.

Dumbstruck and angry, the Nazi then drew
a pistol from his waist. "You female Jew!
You pretended to be worn out, wan and weak?
Then you dare to slap an Aryan cheek?"

He pulled out his gun, aimed and shot at her.
Luckily, he missed. Lotte lurched in fear.
She became a shield between Edith and her killer,
begging and pleading that he please forgive her.

"My sister's pains have made her crazy.
Spare her please. Her mind is hazy."
Lotte calmed him but he wanted to wreak
his punishment on Edith for slapping his cheek.

His expression began to dangerously harden.
The whole family joined in to beg his pardon.
"Her senses have failed her and so she did it.
It shall never happen again. God forbid it."

Hugo and Felix offered recompenses.
"We promise to bring her to her senses."
A depraved punishment the man devised after
he grimaced, and let out a sadistic laughter.

Revolting Retribution

"Start slapping your sister," bellowed the brute.
"Slap the bitch left and right . . . or else I'll shoot.
You must keep slapping her ugly face
until I have fully avenged my disgrace.
The bitch shall be forgiven, if you obey
my command at once . . . start slapping, I say!"

Sybilla intervened. "I know this borders
on outrage, but Lotte please obey his orders."
With weird feelings, Lotte was assailed.
She realized the consequences if she failed.
"I hate what I have to do. Edith knows . . .
she will forgive me after he goes."

Her eyes went blank. Her senses blurred.
As in a nightmarish fog she heard
her hands mechanically slap and slap.
With each strike, the man echoed his clap.
Rapturously the villain was beating time.
Clapping along with the rhythms of his crime.

He would clap and order to slap even harder.
"I'll shoot you both if you don't soothe my ardor.
She would be dead, but you all intervened . . .
so keep slapping, bitch!" ordered this fiend.
When the sisters were exhausted, he was satisfied.
After he left, they both embraced and cried.

Heart-breaking Farewells

All that night the couples lay forlorn
for come tomorrow, they would be torn
away from each other. Love physically deferred,
shall sustain spiritually. Its echoes will be heard.

"Love creates its own heaven. Felix and I
will continue communicating. Love cannot die."
The bonds that welded Felix and Lotte
transcended time to embrace eternity.

"Lovers never die. No one can kill us.
The Greatest Lover of all, God, loves us.
Never in word or deed did you hurt me.
I trust your promise you will never desert me."

Felix promised: "I'll always be by your side.
Without physical proximities, love can thrive.
In spirit I will surely be with you.
You will feel me around in whatever you do."

In another side of the room, broken-hearted,
Edith and Hugo were preparing to be parted.
They held each other with all their might.
Fearing it may be their very last night.

Edith dreaded the impending farewell.
Her fears were real, she could foretell
that this portended something very grim.
She held Hugo tight and cradled him.

Both her daughters' heart-rending good-byes
made Sybilla muffle her sobs, lest her cries
add to her children's pains. She had begun
to love each son-in-law, like her own son.

The following dark and ominous day . . .
as Hugo and Felix were being led away,
Edith, with flailing arms, began to crack,
as she ran after Hugo. Lotte brought her back.

These tragic events Lotte bravely endured
by imagining Felix running back. An illusion conjured
to blend with reality. The thought softened the impact.
Could the American dreams of the five remain intact?

Lotte felt alone, imprisoned by a padlock.
Her blood froze like ice with this shock.
Reverses in true love are transitory.
This was the unshakeable faith of Lotte.

Mother's Health Deteriorates

Sybilla was weakening, she became very pale.
The terrible tragedies were telling their tale.
When old parents weaken, they are in need
of help from their children who owe them indeed.

Ungrateful children can conveniently forget
that parental sacrifices helped them beget
their gifts of life. When parents need them
should children not reciprocate similarly then?

Good and grateful children do not forget
the roles their parents played. This very facet
returns for them to face, so they must understand
this life's cycle, when they too will need a helping hand.
A parent's floundering fortunes must not dim
the memories of when they gave to the brim.
Parents love selflessly and will not think twice
if their children need them for any sacrifice.

Sisters Share Fate

Then another list of deportees came.
It unfortunately included Lotte's name.
The prospect impaled them. Their hearts were stirred.
All day long, the three hardly breathed a word.

Then Edith spoke, "Mother, Lotte cannot go
by herself alone. We cannot throw
her to these wolves." Edith begged and she got
herself included to share her sister's lot.

"Edith, why are you inviting suicide?"
"My place, dear Lotte, is by your side.
Let death come head on, I shall face it.
To protect my little sister, I can embrace it.

We have been together a lifetime through,
the best and the worst. I cannot leave you.
I am your sister, guardian and best friend.
That's what I'll be until the very end.
Remember when neighbors asked me one day
to lend you to them so they could play?
I refused because, Lotte, you were my doll.
You are still very precious. I don't trust them at all."

Edith and Lotte were together taken.
Mother was helpless, crushed and shaken.
With all her children gone, Sybilla started
wailing: "We have been cruelly parted."

She had premonitions deep in every pore
that this separation was forever more.
As this terrible truth began to dawn
on this helpless old widow – she was forlorn.

A Mother's Loss of Children

With hundreds of others, in livestock vans
the sisters were herded. Barbaric Nazi plans
packed them tight like branded cattle.
This suffocating journey tested their mettle.

Were they being lead into a snare?
They were too crushed to even care.
By hunger and thirst, everyone was overcome.
Afraid of the unknown, their senses were numb.

Standing for days, without any sleep,
the weaker ones dropped into a heap.
After the dreaded journey they were led
out of the vans, dazed and half-dead.

"*Out*, you roaches," a Nazi's shout
made them shiver. "You swines, come out!"
They piled out meekly like goats and sheep.
Staggering like zombies from lack of sleep.

They thought the soldiers were maybe too drunk
to notice their dogs tearing chunk after chunk
of flesh from the new arrivals, all numb as ice.
The dogs ripped their flesh, slice after slice.

They arrived in Auschwitz to a grim fate.
"Arbiet macht frei," was inscribed on its gate.
It promised freedom – but it was a grave.
Survival meant existing like a bonded slave.

For a selection, they all had to stand.
Lotte held tight to her sister's hand.
Edith was too weak . . . of all energy bereft.
"Women and children, line up on the left.
Able-bodied ones must stand on the right.
You, *let go*! Don't hold her hand tight!"

Mengle screamed: "Release her hand!"
"She is my sister, Sir, please understand."
"There are no sisters or mothers here.
We are your masters and that better be clear.
Everyone! Be it wife, son or daughter,
who dares disobey, we shall slaughter."

"Please be kind to my sister, Sir,
she joined me for the selfless love in her."
"Tell that to your Jewish God. All your piety . . .
is worthless here just like your religion's deity.
In our Fuhrer's glory, we Germans bask.
Fulfilling his needs is our sacred task."
Mengle was scornful and cold-hearted.
Lotte and Edith were viciously parted.

Tools of Tyrants

His haranguing continued: "Our superior birth
ordains us to eliminate low life on earth.
The world shall witness by Hitler's grace
how we Aryans emerge as the master race."

As they pulled Edith away, Lotte cried,
"I told you sister, you should not have tried
to include your name to be by my side.
I hope your love is not your suicide."

Edith smiled sadly while being taken away
from her sister . . . as if she had wanted to say,
"Sisters are never torn apart, Lotte dear,
our bond shall survive . . . so do not fear."

That night was dark. It began to rain.
Lotte bundled with others, felt a stab of pain.
They were all taken to a bizarre destination.
A bustling bathhouse like a crowded station.

They shaved their heads. They made them kneel.
Then they poured hot water – skins began to peel.
The torture was painful as it was unreal.
Was Edith also suffering a similar ordeal?

A Nazi bellowed, "Remove all clothes and shoes."
Another held his nose. "These filthy Jews!"
The third rasped, "How the Jews exude
a sickly odor when they are in the nude."

Lotte began sinking trying to remain conscious.
She paid no attention to all their obnoxious
slanders and abuse. She was taken to a bunk.
There, in a death-like slumber, she sunk.

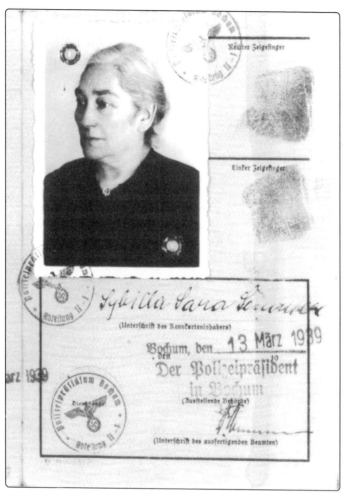

Sybilla Sara Sommers (maiden name: Cohen) was born in Germany on 17th of July, 1871. She wanted to flee the land of her birth as early as 1939 because she sensed the danger that her beloved family could face from the flames of religious persecution.

Death of a Mother

Sybilla's grief was unbearable. Her acute pain
of being parted from her children made her refrain
from eating or drinking. She would cry and moan.
A sorrowful picture of a mother left alone.

Her body weakened daily with deep regret.
Her pitiable condition made many eyes wet.
Some marveled at her spirit, others thought her mad.
Without her children, she was sore and sad.

Mourning silently without vital fluids inside
and without any food . . . Sybilla quietly died.
A splendid light was shining from her eyes.
It was her vision of a reunion in paradise.

Her body was dumped in an unmarked hole.
From her wounds there beamed an indomitable soul.
Her corpse lay in squalor, but in heaven's grace
God welcomed Sybilla with a warm embrace.

Hope for the Hopeless

What does not kill only makes us stronger.
No one does physically suffer longer
than their tolerance level. When pains go beyond
endurance . . . we lose consciousness. God does respond!

He has wisely implanted in each creation
devices that deliver the needed alleviation
of unbearable pains. These faculties bestow
an etherized state so victims will not know.

With His creations, He has a caring bond.
God gifted us freewill. He will not respond
to each thorn prick but eventually takes control
to judiciously elevate or downgrade a soul.

Many people are obsessed with material benefits.
The enlightened seek out horizons without limits.
Those with fleeting fortunes cannot console
their seared spirits if they have sold their soul.

Death of a Sister

One morning with a foreboding Lotte awoke.
Her first and only words that she spoke
were: "Kindly tell me, has anyone seen
my sister Edith. Where has she been?
She was taken . . . I don't know where.
Please help me find her, because I care
more for her than for myself. I hope she fled
this brutal camp and is not dead."

A guard mockingly said: "You have missed her
by a few moments. Look! There see your sister
flying with our flames and smoke to applaud
your weak and helpless Jewish God."

With no compassion, feelings or even tact,
he sadistically boasted about this fact.
Drunk by the heady power of a Nazi dress
he loved to trample, rule and repress.

"Jews are the chosen people, you all had bragged.
Yet, you are fated to be crushed and dragged
by us, your masters. You will see how we stamp
your foolish boasts in our concentration camp."

Like a slave Lotte worked despite fragile bones.
To pave Nazi roads she had to break stones.
Vulgar jests, jeers and merciless beatings,
was the ruthless mode of Nazi greetings.

She wished for death. It was denied to her.
She suffered tortures and gnawing hunger.
Praying and pleading she cried out in grief,
"My dear kind Lord . . . I need some relief!"

Was it a reverie or was it real? She was invited
into Felix's warm arms . . . they were united.
He whispered in her ears clear and loud:
"Be a winner, Lotte, and make me proud."

Felix revived her. She felt strong again.
The whispers of his voice relieved her pain.
Were these merely her hallucinations?
Love is able to tap the divine dimensions.

What is real existence? The mortal or divine?
With true love Lotte erased this dividing line.
Her love for Felix made it imperative
that her life must propound only the positive.

The perimeters and fetters alienating our mind,
from spiritual realms can be left behind
when the gossamer veils lift – all divinity is yours.
Material focuses obscure the eternal doors.

An Out-of-Body Experience

Alas, in Auschwitz, Lotte arduously existed.
To backbreaking chores she was constantly shifted.
A guard's lewd remarks created a quagmire.
"I find you attractive in your tattered attire."

She cringed with fear and shook with ire.
Was he harboring some sordid desire?
To overcome this, Lotte visualized Felix's arm
wrap around her to protect her from harm.

The guard then made a shocking proposition.
She rejected it at once with a firm opposition.
He threatened her furiously. "Go to that barn!
You have a job to do." She knew it was a yarn.

Lust loomed large in the rascal's eyes.
She knew that no one would hear her cries.
"I shall have you killed, if you disobey."
Lotte was helpless – there was no other way.

Obediently she followed, her heart quivering.
From head to toe her body was shivering.
She entered the barn very numb and sore.
He shoved her in and slammed the door.
"Please, Sir, I am married, it would be awful
if to my husband I became unfaithful."

"Remove your clothes, woman! Every shred.
Let me see you get undressed!
First, I want to enjoy, your bosom's delight.
Do your breasts droop or are they upright?
Drop your dress down to your slender waist.
Nice and slow . . . and don't make haste.
Slither it slowly down to your thighs.
Slide it lower, let me feast my eyes.
Next I am going to be deep inside.
Lie down and spread your legs real wide."

"Please, Sir, please don't. Let me go!"
The beast struck Lotte a stunning blow
almost cracking her skull with his rifle butt.
She collapsed and her eyes sagged shut.

Redefining Reality

"My Felix arrived as soon as he found
me in trouble. My abductor in profound
fear began to flee. Happy to be free,
I ran to my husband in great glee.

Maybe this guard was from the tribe
who helped Felix by taking a bribe
to arrange our meeting. My Felix was hungry
for me and had to resort to this trickery.

As if in a trance (but almost crystal clear),
despite my head wound, I could feel and hear
Felix holding and caressing me once again.
This was no dream, I saw him plain.

He held me with passion in his arms
then showered me with all his charms.
Beyond the physical interaction
I focused on the spirit and emotion.

His lips locked passionately on my own
to smother me with kisses. I heard him groan.
No other man would I let or could ever
spiral me to passion's heightened fever.

Flights of feminine fantasy, although mild,
can sometimes make women crave for a wild
adventure . . . to unleash the floodgates
of flaming passions with their mates.

Now maybe for Felix such a need returned.
Alcohol had made him wildly impassioned.
I recalled our honeymoon's fond memory.
Was it happening again or was it a reverie?

Did Felix once again drink too much?
I felt the same wild kiss and touch.
As he moved and rocked over my body
my tears began flowing and I felt giddy.

His passion exploded. I heard him roar.
Like a satiated lion and then no more.
He got off and left . . . nay, literally fled.
Leaving me alone, half-alive, half-dead."

Deception or Denial?

"Felix fled from our tryst, I thought,
to escape the dangers of being caught.
I returned to my stinking barracks where
Margie, my friend, was in deep despair.
She disbelieved whatever I spoke."
"Are you delirious, Lotte, or is this a joke?
You'll go insane if you do not shed
your imaginary rendezvous," Margie said.

"Your head injuries made you fantasize you escaped.
Thus you are in denial of having been raped.
Our mind is capable of making us feel
that illusions are true by distorting the real."

To escape the trauma of such villainy
women resort to mentally altering reality.
Time heals wounds, but will also wound a heel.
Wrongdoers ultimately pay for what they steal.

A woman's body offers so much more . . .
love and tenderness reside in its core.
The rapists are not victors when they stain
this sacred temple. They are losers and insane.

This span of life is a transient mist.
Ultimately only our souls shall exist.
If we sustain our spirits through a calamity,
we shall be rewarded with God's proximity.
Lotte thus cleared life's murky swamp.
Her unsoiled spirit was her triumph.

"They cannot crush me for I insist
their delusions are tendrils of a smoky mist.
Beyond this flesh, my bones and pores,
in eternal realms, Felix, I am *only* yours."

Lotte's Motivation

"After I discovered this treasure trove,
Hans, I wanted to share insights of love
with the readers – not for fortune or fame.
Nor do I write to extol my name.

I want my gems of wisdom to reach
remote corners of this world to all and each . . .
helpless women and innocent children
who are victims of any heartless heathen.

The lessons of my life can defeat tyranny.
The armor of love is mightier than villainy.
Cultures of violence and their strangleholds
masquerade in garbs of religious blindfolds.

Maybe for this mission I did not die.
Through dreadful disasters I scraped by.
God wanted me to help His needy children.
Each child is a precious flower of His garden.
Creations of all colors, class, creed or race
were created by Him. Each has a special place.

He gifts us children to brighten our future.
Religious fanatics subject them to torture.
The flood of tears from a mother's eyes
can drown despots. God watches from the skies.

The expectations held by the heavens above
of human beings, is to accentuate love.
The gifts God gave to the human race
were meant to make earth a better place."

Wheels of Justice

The perpetrators soon faced their own holocaust.
War after war, which they waged, was being lost.
Their atrocities and demoniac repressions
had already surpassed existing dimensions.

Their Day of Judgment rolled on its way.
Ultimately all criminals have to pay.
For every evil deed there is a price.
Penalties shall be added to deter vice.

The Russians began avenging the very hard
blows the Germans dealt to Stalingrad.
Under the onslaught of Russia's armor of steel,
panic besieged the Nazis, they began to reel.

A Trial of Tears

Auschwitz, the camp all prisoners hated,
was very hastily being evacuated.
To cover up evidence was their endeavor.
In desperation, they became even meaner.

The prisoners prayed for a Russian victory
to escape their misery and be free.
The Nazis leveraged their ruthless will.
Thus the prisoners' dreams amounted to nil.

From one camp to another they were led.
The walking skeletons, the living dead.
The old or crippled, who moved wearily,
were killed by the Nazis mercilessly.

The Germans fled as countless hordes
of Russians arrived with guns and swords.
Their war machine was fully empowered.
Each Nazi trembled like a cringing coward.

With unrelenting cruelty they callously told
their prisoners to sleep out in the cold.
The only means to keep a little warm
was to huddle in groups they began to form.

"A little raw milk they finally fed us
lest we die of hunger. Yet were generous
with their tortures. My strength – there was none.
Then Felix's voice echoed: 'Lotte keep on.'

Behind a wagon train, abandoned and small,
we were permitted to answer nature's call.
They expected us to hail their civility,
for offering this very basic facility.

From one camp to the next with tired feet,
blistered and bleeding and trudging through sleet,
the wounds of most prisoners left blotches of red.
The white snow, it seemed, had blistered and bled."

Eloquent Indictments

The sick and hungry died day and night.
Wayside corpses were a familiar sight.
These macabre war trophies were strewn and lain.
Each victim's soul shall haunt every villain.

Through biting cold and stinging sleet
prisoners wore wooden clogs on their feet.
The pangs of hunger began to grow.
Lotte sought some relief by eating snow.

When the Nazis felt a few should be fed,
some lucky ones got a sausage and bread.
Before Lotte could eat a woman grabbed
all of her food and, like a thief, she fled.

Lotte wanted to chase her but she heard
the echo of a voice. From Felix she learned:
"Her need was greater. My beloved, please treat
her plight with compassion. Life is bitter-sweet."

Lotte found the 'culprit' who was feeding
her starving child . . . she began pleading
with tear-filled eyes: "My baby was hungry."
It was so heart-rending. Lotte was not angry.

Death-Wish

Lotte was jealous of Eva, a very broken girl,
who staggered along but one day in a swirl
she fell flat on her face. Plunged into a sleep
that was timeless, fathomless and deep.

Eva's death surprisingly began to bestir,
strange desires in Lotte. She envied her!
The meek gracefully accept and are not sorry,
when death takes them to their greater glory.

The proud and the powerful lament and grieve,
to hear death's call. For they have to leave
what they hoarded here. They ignored the fact
that earthy goods never remain intact.

The plundering murderers did not care.
They shaved heads of victims for their hair.
How long can such harvests last?
Life's ill-gotten gains begin to rot fast.

A Stone Melts

Lotte had collapsed on a heap of snow.
She lost consciousness and seemed as though
the heat and cold were simultaneously being felt.
Felix intervened, else death would have been dealt.

His help came as a blow from a soldier's gun
brought Lotte back from her peaceful oblivion.
The Nazi hit her hard like a snarling brute.
Then aimed his gun . . . all ready to shoot!

Through blurred visions she saw that this guard
had kinder eyes though his posture was hard.
She saw a glimmer of Felix in his face -
her husband now stood in the soldier's place.

"Beloved Lotte, please do understand
that you must not die. Now rise and stand
to surmount each adversity. The brave don't run."
Then she saw the soldier pull back his gun.

The soldier told Lotte, "Lady, kindly forgive
my waking you up. I heard that you must live
by some strange whispers from the skies.
Is something wrong with my ears or eyes?"

At the sky and Lotte he gazed in awe.
Lotte replied in clear German without a flaw,
"It was a divine revelation," she said.
He asked, "Need some coffee and bread?
I am risking my life and my position
by helping you, but I must mention
that a spirit seems to swirl around you.
Its echoes emanated from the blue.
I was told that for many years still
you must live . . . you have a destiny to fulfill."

"Felix used the soldier as a medium for his voice.
Our connection is intact. I must rejoice."
Cosmic links with Felix breathed the power
to believe that lovers need never cower.
True love can energize a very frail life
and make it conquer insurmountable strife.

Let villains do their worst, they will never succeed.
With love as a weapon the lovers are freed,
(from man-made shackles), to tread above
evil forces . . . since God favors love!

For this energy emanates from God Himself.
It is infinitely greater than all this world's pelf.
Lotte felt Felix's love in her every breath.
That's how she overcame the traps of death.

By stoking the religious or an ideological fire,
rage is whipped up to convert the ire
of the weak-willed who become hateful brutes.
Brainwashed, they strap on marching boots.

The puppeteers, after victory do also betray
those puppets who helped them find the way.
The dogmas they propounded: "Terror is right",
projects the devil's darkness and not divine light.

Glimmers of God

A voice from above boomed: *"You are my daughter,*
like my many other children these sinners slaughter.
Your ordeals shall be rewarded. Lotte, you will find
that nothing escapes my ears, eyes or mind.
Of all the creations that I have made,
the meek and weak should be least afraid.
To the sinners who perpetrate crime
I shall respond suitably at a proper time."

Was it a dream? To verify, Lotte cast
her vision on to the heavens so vast.
Her gloom dispelled for she began to hear
her own father's voice echoing in her ear.

"Dear daughter, your plight is painfully strange.
Your ultimate parent, God, shall bring about change.
Hold on to your faith in the meanwhile."
Her father spoke with wisdom and a smile.

Adolph Sommer's words warmed the icy chill.
It boosted and bolstered her weakening will.
She rebelled against the job of breaking stones.
For the task was verily wreaking her bones.

When she declared this, everyone was aghast.
No prisoner had survived rebellion in the past.
Anyone insane enough to challenge their lot
was mercilessly punished or else just shot.

With a rigid resolve, Lotte took a stand.
Defiantly dropping the tools in her hand.
When they saw her rebellious spirit rise,
her guards gaped with disbelieving eyes.

The Lamb and The Lion

One soldier aimed at her. Lotte was too tired.
She couldn't care less if the soldier fired.
"My faith teaches me to never fear death,
so soldier, I dare you to snuff out my breath.
This body my parents had so lovingly caressed,
was a temple for my husband's happiness and rest.
From my childhood, it blossomed like a flower
and exuded pure love every sunlit hour.
The lullabies of death you oppressors would hum
did devastate humanity and many did succumb."

"Get back to work," the soldier screamed out loud.
He spoke in German with a posture so proud.
His demeanor definitely revealed the level
of his mindless devotion as disciple of the devil.
To his robotic command Lotte boldly replied
in German, a language of great pride:

"Soldier, delve into your soul and defy
evil orders of the despots. Let Hitler try
to demonize German people . . . why should you
help him in his sins by shooting this Jew?

My father and grandfather had bravely fought,
for Germany in World War I and never thought,
that Germans would one day begin to choose
fellow Germans for torture, just for being Jews?

Despots do brainwash but what is really odd,
is to see intelligent people devoted to this clod.
Those who kill another human are really stupid.
Take my life, if you believe Hitler created it.

A careful crafting of schemes with dramatics,
enable the tyrants to recruit their fanatics.
I was born in Germany too, just like you.
The only difference – I was born a Jew."

The soldier glared at Lotte throughout her tirade.
Her frail arms flailed – she was not afraid.
An epiphany pierced deep and to everyone's surprise,
profuse tears came rolling from the soldier's eyes.

He began to tremble overcome by emotion.
Many realize, too late, that a mindless devotion
facilitates megalomaniacs in their sinful deeds.
Many innocent lives are lost to these breeds.

They run regimes in a ruthless way.
Repression and suppression helps them sway
forces to control. Yet 'Amazing Grace' may
after proper repentance, wash their sins away.

The soldier was also some mother's beloved son.
Lotte wished constructive tools would replace his gun.
It is very possible for redemption to be attained.
Many a sinner has reformed to become a saint.

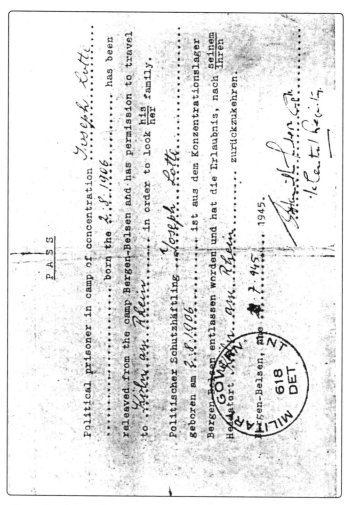

Copy of 1945 certificate, which allowed Lotte a short relief from Bergen-Belsen concentration camp. The ravaged interns were euphemistically referred to as "Political Prisoners."

Twisting in the Wind

At Bergen-Belsen camp where they were taken.
Lotte's hands were bleeding, her feet were swollen.
What more did they want, these masters of crime?
To splatter more blood on the face of time?

Lotte was awakened at the stroke of five.
She trembled in the cold. Many did not survive
the daily hauling out from their dingy shack,
then toiling in the stupor of a routine so black.

Forced labor made them shiver in the cold.
Faint warmth emanated from the sun's rays of gold.
Seeing man's inhumanity to man so replete,
the sun seemed hesitant to radiate heat.

On either side of Lotte, Hazel and Mariam slept.
That is how each one of them kept
the other warm. One night a touch of cold skin
made Lotte feel faint and her head spin.

Was she unconscious or did she in her sleep
lapse into a coma that was very deep?
To help the helpless, God lovingly dispenses
means to anaesthetize the pained senses.

When Lotte awoke, she was trembling with awe
at the sight that greeted her. She sadly saw
Hazel and Mariam being carried away.
They had died. Lotte began to pray:

"Dear Hazel and Mariam, victims of life's error,
you have liberated yourselves from this terror.
I thank you for the warmth you gave me in bed.
The cold will remind me that you are dead.
Starvation did not kill but I think your will
was shattered by the merciless, cruel chill.
We shared lice and cold nights together.
You have left me now to continue to suffer.
Echoes from beyond help me to conquer
evil energies. Without them, I could falter."

From all of her horrors, typhus was the worst.
This ailment can bring on unbearable thirst.
Lotte saw what she had never ever seen.
Thirsts were being quenched with urine!

Without water or food they were lying
gasping for breath and painfully dying.
Lotte prayed for someone to wet her lip.
She longed and thirsted for just a sip.

Lotte soothed her pain by shifting her focus.
She imagined nature's bounties open like a lotus
that took her to gardens with buttercups and daffodils.
She savored their exquisite aromas and other frills.

Couples beautified her world with bridal glitter
dancing to the raptures of birdsongs and twitter.
Birds of all colors were flying here and there.
Sweet sparkling water cascaded everywhere.

Leaves rustled with cool whispers of the breeze
flowing and fluttering between branches and trees.
Like a chorus, Felix, Edith, Hugo and her mother
sang sweet melodies to make her feel better.

People's power to imagine is God's gift to escape
the unbearable with an imaginary drape.
To be able to do this can be helpful no doubt.
Inherent defense mechanisms prevent being fraught.

Hans Harangues Again

"Lotte and Mickey, I know what drives you.
Let me try to express it poetically too.
Every day, all the time, these spiritual smuts
which you spiel on and on, are driving me nuts.
I feel you both are simply pretending.
This afterlife fixation is merely sending
false hopes to people. This fabled stuff,
like witchery and voodoo, is only a bluff."

Lotte responded with a sharp zinger.
She trumped Hans with the following stinger:
"Good try, Hans, but your cynical banter
against our beliefs is quite off-center.

My faith in existence beyond the body
kindles divine strength when people are ready
to bid final good-byes . . . they can smile.
Afterlife, Hans, is our ultimate domicile.

If worth is measured by material wealth alone,
then does its loss mean life's value is gone?
Our worth becomes infinite with spiritual wings
for with them we can access eternal springs.

Hans, if you are not yet ready to agree,
we can move on by agreeing to disagree.
When arguments meander and become futile,
we should stop arguing and share a smile."

A compromise in different beliefs can occur,
if open-minded perceptions and tolerance concur.
Nothing should be rejected with a curt smother.
The issues return to haunt sometime or another.
Love can flourish despite a difference.
God blesses acts of charitable jurisprudence.

How Lotte Survived the War

After Hazel and Mariam died, Lotte felt a snake
coiled tight on her chest to kept her awake.
Without their warmth for the rest of her days
she slept in the cold grips of a dizzy haze.

One day she witnessed through the floating mist,
a strange scene of being carried into the midst
of a pile of corpses. Was she dead or alive?
It was April 15, 1945.

British soldiers facilitated their liberation.
It was a moment of great celebration.
Someone noticed that Lotte was still breathing.
The alerted medics immediately began hustling.

Twilight Zones

Through half open eyes, Lotte saw a light.
It was very different – pure and angelic white.
At first she thought it was another set of dreams.
A diaphanous curtain filtered the beams.

White uniforms and clean sheets on her bed
made her wonder if she was really dead.
Doctors immediately began to administer
medical treatment and her body began to stir.

These alien comforts in which she lay
disoriented her. She heard herself say,
"My husband arranged this, as he promised.
But where is my Felix, my eternal beloved?"

These were Felix's fulfilled promises, she knew.
Better late than never, he always came through.
"I missed you, Felix. Without you my pain
was unbearable. Don't leave me again!"

Then she heard his voice, it could not be clearer.
"My darling Lotte, even death cannot sever
two lovers like us whose bonds were spun
by eternity's sturdy threads. Love has won!
You will be triumphant. All those very rotten
tortures of the past shall soon be forgotten."

Their reunion went beyond a cuddle or caress.
They connected in zones that were timeless.
Felix's passionate kisses and tight embrace
evaporated Lotte's pains for an ultimate solace.
This was what she had long yearned for . . .
Celestial ecstasy like the days of yore.

Then Felix began to vaporize into thin air.
"Stop!" she shouted. "It's not right and fair.
I've waited so long. How much I have pined."
But once more, she was sadly left behind.

She screamed at heaven from where Felix came.
Imagination and reality melded to look the same.
She wondered if heaven had conspired with hell.
Then on the floor, unconscious, she fell.

Altered States of Mind

The medicinal smells hung like a cloud.
They assailed her nostrils. She cried aloud.
"I don't belong in hell. The masked men lifted
me here by mistake. I must be shifted.
Please get me out of this ridiculous mix.
I'll find my heaven in the arms of Felix."

Without him Lotte felt nothing was well.
"Am I surrounded by my enemies in hell?
Did Hitler invade heaven with his villainous crew?"
What was real or illusion she no longer knew.

God designed her birth for her to belong
to the Jewish race. What did *she* do wrong?
She hollered like the deranged and demented;
her chase after 'Felix' . . . the nurses prevented.

Then she collapsed into a deep repose.
Unconscious to the world until she arose
to the odor of iodine and chloroform's smell.
She figured she had probably landed in hell.

Doctors and nurses held her by force.
"You need intense treatment, of course!
Medicine, as you know, is not a magic wand.
Look at yourself, you can hardly stand!"

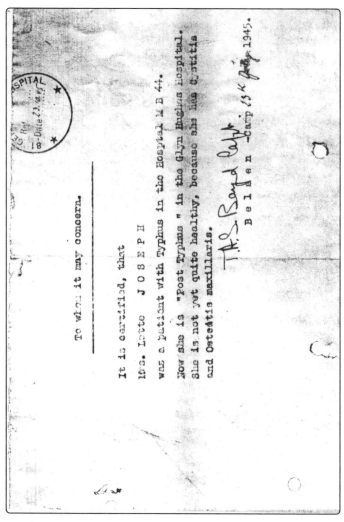

To whom it may concern.

It is certified, that

Mrs. Lotte J O S E P H

was a patient with Typhus in the Hospital N D 44.

Now she is "Post Typhus" in the Glyn Hughes Hospital. She is not yet quite healthy, because she has Cystitis and Osteitis maxillaris.

T.A.S. Raynd Cuff
B e l s e n Camp 13 th July 1945.

Resident medical officer at the liberated Glyn Hughes Hospital certifies that Lotte was too sick to be freed.

Her laser sharp focus beamed only for
Felix, her husband and eternal lover.
She could not wait. She was in grief.
So she made her escape like a thief.

She stealthily crawled towards the exit.
There in a mirror she saw every bit
of her deep sunken eyes devoid of lashes.
All over her body were red marks of slashes.

She fell screaming on her hands and knees.
It caught the attention of the nurses and orderlies.
They came and dragged her to a bed
and securely pinned her to the bedstead.
She cried, "Why are you being so inhuman
by keeping a man away from his woman?"

She then appealed to God, "Please tell us,
why lovers are separated – are people jealous?
They would be magnanimous if only they knew
of the splendor of eternal love like Felix and I do.
Then they would release me immediately, no doubt.
Please God, teach them what love is all about."

The doctors felt that she be sedated.
Her befuddled delirium later abated.
A doctor gently told her, "You must wait.
You cannot get leave until you recuperate."

He instructed the nurses, "She must recover
before she is allowed to tryst with her lover."
Lotte's love for Felix made her out of control.
Failed physical fulfillments buffeted her soul.

Dawning of Decency

Slowly on Germany peace descended.
Tyrants were vanquished, their tyranny ended.
Adolph Hitler's oratory was now hushed.
His sinister plans were completely crushed.

Every despot including his disciples and friends
shall find their evil actions come to similar ends.
Those who for others prepare a poison cup
inevitably end up having to drink it up.

History cautions that revisions of world maps,
imposed by force, are unacceptable mishaps.
The vanquished will win and brutes shall depart.
Victories don't last if they break people's heart.

Tryst of Lovers

Most people who had been liberated
from concentration camps, soon migrated.
Felix had promised their tryst near a bank.
Lotte waited daily, but drew a blank.

She stood there searching, hoping to trace
amidst the milling crowds her beloved's face.
Each day she was hopeful. Lurking fears
of failure would fill her eyes with tears.
He always kept his word. Her faith was lush.
With outstretched arms one day he'll rush
to hold her in his arms. Hopeful ears heard:
"I am back Lotte. I have kept my word."

Only with Felix could completeness
return to replace her sad emptiness.
Daily Lotte diligently hitched her camp.
In the pursuits of love, she was a champ.

She heard God's voice. He made her know:
"Human horrors, Lotte, will come and go.
The worth of bad people's soul shall shrink.
Your values and deeds are enhancing our link.
For being patient, forgiving and resourceful,
you are priming your soul to be eternally blissful."

This divine wisdom made her discover
the supreme insights she needed to recover.
Each helpless cry is heard by the Divine.
God responds in His own good time.

In positive attitudes there breeds a state
of mind and spirit that can eclipse hate.
Charitable and humane traits behoove a person.
Looking beyond the immediate self propels evolution.

Our hearts can become a home of charity
by sympathizing with people's bouts of insanity.
Moments of madness can afflict the best of us.
Untreated psychosis is very dangerous.

The perils of autocracy is that mental maladies
of a single individual can cause millions of tragedies.
Absolute power is fertile ground for vices.
A checks and balance system can prevent crises.

Survival Strategies

When waiting for Felix, she felt was in vain,
the doubts arose, "Shall we meet again?"
Discounting her own doubts, she hopefully said,
"I am a fool to think that he could be dead.
Maybe he suffered something cruel, I dread.
Or he's disoriented by a blow on his head.
I have full faith that he will ultimately return . . .
for traumas can often make people taciturn."

Jews from Germany migrated far away.
Lotte heard that many went to the U.S.A.
She pondered and thought the chances were fair
to assume or believe that Felix might be there.

Lotte's hopes revived all over again . . .
patience in love is never in vain.
"Please help me reach the United States."
She begged her friends and begged her mates.

Where Dreams are Fulfilled

All on the ship were excited when they neared
the shores of U.S.A. Everybody cheered.
Etched against the dim horizon Lotte could see
a stately gentle lady: The Statue of Liberty.

America's free society allays people's fears.
But Lotte's eyes were filled with tears.
Memories assailed her. She began to remember
her beloved lost family – each, a missing passenger.
As the ship sailed on through inclement weather,
she visualized all the five who had dreamed together.
Both Edith and Hugo she saw stand
near Felix and herself all hand-in-hand.

Sybilla was exuding love and motherly grace.
Each one glowed with a happy smiling face.
Mother said ecstatically, "Now for me and you,
in America, a life of happiness begins anew.
My beloved children, my very own,
now please don't ever leave me alone."

Lotte saw Edith counting the crates
that she had packed for the United States.
She had packed well so their life on earth,
would no longer suffer a sense of dearth.
When agonies are acute, imaginations run wild.
Lotte began dancing like a joyful child.

The great Lady Liberty whose grace illumined
the lives of so many, for Lotte now shined
a light of sublime love. "She is embracing me.
Am I imagining my family or is this reality?"

From that warmth she could clearly discern
that in America she may never be alone.
Lotte deduced that Felix had already arrived.
Her dormant hopes were now amplified.

Scattered Dreams

"How many family members have come with you?"
The immigration officer's formal question drew
a flood of tears. The officer was taken aback.
"His question, like a hammer blow, made my head crack.
My body began trembling. I began to fall.
The astonished officer made me sit in the hall."

"Ignore my question. You are like my daughter.
Don't cry please, drink a glass of water."
"Kind officer, Sir, all my family is lost.
We were victims of the grim holocaust.
But my husband survived . . . I have come for him.
My mother, Edith and Hugo's fate was grim.
I am all alone, is my answer to your question.
Searching for my husband is my main mission.
Our wonderful group of five was torn apart.
But I confess, they are with me in my heart."

Keeping Hope Alive

Immigration records and every which way,
Lotte searched for Felix, both night and day.
Few disappointments a resolve do not derail.
"Where are you Felix?" was her anguished wail.

Love can crown but it can also crucify.
Lovers fare better than those who never try.
People in love won't hesitate to pay any price.
Valuable gains do not come without sacrifice.

Friends and relatives dissuaded her, yet
she refused to believe that Felix could forget.
She would often go near arriving ships and wait.
Many called her crazy or plain obstinate.

Was it hope that helped her to stay alive?
Without hope, could she ever survive?
"Life without Felix is a living death.
I'll wait for him until my last breath."

If denial can be a constructive device
to help people cope, then the only advice
is to apply it judiciously . . . not in an overdose.
Does denial help? One could suppose!

To pay for her needs and a roof over her head,
Lotte looked for work and soon was blessed.
Her hand-to-mouth existence, a major malady,
failed to dampen the spirits of this lady.

Sincerity of purpose makes people strong-hearted.
With single-minded tenacity, courage is imparted.
She buried her grief in chores, routine and formal,
because total immersion facilitates being normal.

Human Resilience

Lotte accepted the opportunities America did offer.
Her hard work and goodness made her prosper.
It is a land of vitality but nevertheless,
how do the lovelorn cure their loneliness?

Time spent in love and honor of commitment
will flood a home with sweet fulfillment.
If parents are too busy and children are neglected -
it is difficult to heal the scars of being rejected.
The house is not a home, if it is like a racecourse.
It breeds resentment, increasing chances of divorce.

People become insensitive or even insane
if they obsessively pursue a hollow gain.
Whatever earth offers, comes to naught.
Sans spiritual sustenance, life is distraught.

Materialistic love can be hectic and confounded.
Its fickle flavor is fleeting, so no one is bonded.
Grabbing and hoarding at a frantic pace
hurts the body and spirit. It's a rueful rat race.
Is it worthwhile becoming a champion rat
and lose the tranquility of a spiritual habitat?

Spiritual gains and goals are the paradigm.
Far-sighted wisdom shall see them as our prime
purpose on earth. Diversions dilute contentment
and bring on frustration, so Lotte was different.

She stood tall like a steeple . . .
and inspired so many people.
Her soul was suffused with sublime tranquility
because she did everything with selfless sincerity.

Hope Springs Eternal

Edith's heavenly whispers were very distinct.
"Lotte, the loneliness that has linked
itself to you shall very soon cease.
Beloved sister, you shall find peace."

Was Edith right? Were the words she spoke
prophetic and wise? Her message did evoke
Lotte's hope. It was springtime so she thought
Edith was alluding to the spring Felix brought.

Hope springs eternal, Lotte believed still.
"He must know I miss him. He must now fulfill
my hopes and dreams for no one else can.
Felix was my first and shall be the last man."

Lotte created happiness by recalling celebrations
of her moments of love and Felix's inspirations:
"Beyond human measures or mortal surmise
I love my angel with gypsy green eyes.
Lotte, my body and eternal soul
belong to you. I may not control
this earth, the sun, the moon or a star
but my love follows wherever you are.
Even from heaven, Lotte, forever
my love for you shall never waver."
Lotte dispelled despair by learning to hear
this song as the solo sound in her ear.

Key to Success

Children need a father's love as much a mother's.
It is also welcomed from sisters and brothers.
Fulfillment can come with neighbors and friends.
But the support of a spouse meets all our ends.

Spouses complement each other and can ill-afford
to lose the other. No one in life is more adored
or needed as much. The world grows dim
after losing a spouse . . . life becomes grim.

Lotte translated her grief into song.
Art helps our spirits to remain strong.
Lotte's performances radiated an inner verity.
Her love epitomized selfless sincerity.

Life turns around with hard work and success.
All sincere efforts God will amply bless.
Lotte's spirited singing made her listeners feel
her sweet-n-sublime moods and it helped some heal.

Inspiration is a positive by-product of stress.
Combine it with hard work and it spells success.
Tragedies can be effectively converted
into constructive energies so damage is averted.

From the depths of her soul, Lotte's voice rang.
She stirred her listeners whenever she sang.
The audience profusely applauded and cheered.
As a singer, Lotte was very endeared.

The notes that accompanied her on the cello,
stirred all emotions – the deep and the mellow.
The ingrained pain by which she was torn
smelted into art, to be easier borne.

When love inspires an artist to perform,
it helps to create an emotional storm.
Routinely a large audience swarmed
New York's Columbia Hall, when Lotte performed.

Their clapping and cheering was unabated.
Lotte was effusively praised and congratulated.
If only those who so warmly shook her hand
peered into her heart – they would understand.

Deafening Silence

Her deep despair by the separation of years
from Felix, brought on a film of tears.
This sorrow unknown to the people in the hall
made them conjecture, what she would recall.

"Her husband was killed," someone said.
"No!" Lotte screamed, "He can never be dead.
My Felix cannot die . . . he is divine.
He throbs in every breath of mine."

"You were magnificent," said Dr. Schwartz.
"The way you play piano has won our hearts.
It was a great performance, for in it I see,
the mark and makings of a great destiny."

She listened to what everyone would say . . .
while memories transported her miles away.
Taking her back to her life in Germany,
where she shared her love with so many.

The promises of love that were made,
froze time in its tracks. Memories would cascade.
She'd remember each moment with surreal clarity . . .
her dolls and Edith became tangible reality.

Edith's favorite frock, her family home,
the alluring roadways where they would roam.
The clean cafes, woodlands and fireflies,
glittering at night like angel eyes.

The poison of prejudice made her suffer
horrible tragedies. Her sister would never
return after that cruel, dark, sorrowful day.
She was haunted by Edith being torn away.

Edith's selfless love was what caused her
to be killed so cruelly. Oh, what a sister!
Survivors left behind are plagued by guilt,
even after their life has been rebuilt.
Retribution ripped Germany apart too.
Poetic justice? A country split into two.

Therapy for Love

In those times therapy was the luxury of a few
nouveau riche, the fashionable or well-to-do.
To be crazy in love is not deemed madness.
Intense love touches the realms of excess.

Lotte thought that her therapist was rather sneaky.
He was asking questions that seemed tricky.
She found his enquiries to be very intrusive.
His allusion to Felix's death she found offensive.

"You have a Felix fixation," the doctor declared,
"you'll come down to earth when it is repaired."
Lotte felt this remark went beyond his mandate . . .
love is an emotion that only lovers appreciate.

Her retort to his insistence was a reprimand.
"Healer, heal yourself for failing to understand
that the power of love is a magnificent obsession.
Labeling lovers 'loony' is a misinterpretation.

The mind of a lover is driven by emotion.
'I'm crazy about you' is an accepted notion.
Extreme heights of love are not exaggerations . . .
they are the thresholds to our divine dimensions.

Love cannot be measured nor any calculations
can determine its heights. Mundane assumptions
can never be the measure of our spiritual spectrum."
To Lotte this trite therapy was thus unwelcome.

The sessions of therapy screeched to a halt.
"Please understand, Sir, it is not your fault.
My love for Felix helps me to communicate
beyond your range – love's reach is too great.
I see twinkling stars ride on the back
of our divine love. Our music track . . .
it is eternal, because our echoes of love
make a melody of it in heavens above."

Breaking Racial Barriers

Gloria could, with her sweet delicious voice,
make her listeners marvel and rejoice.
Gifted talent was the greatest of her virtues.
Lotte loved this black singer's stirring muse.

Whenever Gloria sang Lotte was inspired.
By Gloria's golden voice her emotions were fired
to sing heart-rending songs of yester-years.
Lotte's pathos drove the audience to tears.

To David, the promoter, a white woman said,
"One room for two with a bunker bed?
You must respect our views so take care,
a room with Gloria we will not share.
To save you money we accept what you ask.
But sleeping in the same room is an impossible task."

Lotte was angered by such puerile patter.
To her only Gloria's talents did matter.
Against any discrimination, Lotte was intrepid.
"I'll share Gloria's room," she announced to David.
She despised prejudice – having been a victim.
Lotte's offer to David was a relief for him.

Gloria overheard what had been said.
Lotte consoled her: "Some are badly bred
with narrow visions . . . their growth is small.
Forgive them and you will rise above them all."

"You are right, Lotte," Gloria began to say,
"I already feel better than them – any day!"
Lotte's lofty attitude others felt was a bubble.
"It is bound to burst for Gloria spells trouble."

After the show Lotte decided to sleep.
The upper bunker bed was just too steep.
Lotte chose the lower one ardently hoping
to dream of Felix while she was sleeping.

She hoped to be asleep when Gloria would return.
But Gloria had hatched plans to date someone.
Gloria's belief was that hypocrisy and inhibitions
are to free spirits, unwelcome restrictions.

Passions in the Dark

Lotte heard Gloria stealthily opening the latch.
Gloria had planned to make out with her catch.
She tiptoed up to check. Was Lotte awake?
Lotte pretended to sleep. That was her mistake.

Gloria's lover came over when the night was deep.
They had calculated that Lotte would be asleep.
On this presumption, Gloria had relied.
She convinced her man. He was satisfied.

Holding his hand, on tiptoes, she brought
him towards the bed. Lotte was wrought
with so much fear that she did not shake,
or even budge, lest they know she was awake.

The remaining lights of the room were put out.
Gloria whispered to her man, "Sammy, no doubt
when our bodies are bare and enmesh,
sweet steamy passion will engulf our flesh."

Gloria, the gorgeous and glorious singer
could make men dance around her finger.
"Sammy, you are my only lover . . .
rest assured, I have no other.
Lotte sleeps soundly . . . so Sammy, you are
to perform tonight like a superstar.
Make passionate love all night to me.
Thanks to the bunk beds, Lotte can't see.
She sleeps below . . . so *please* beware.
Move your body with utmost care."

Gloria's claims were wrong, more like a joke.
Lotte clearly heard whatever they spoke.
"Sweet Gloria, you are my honey cup."
"Prove it, Sammy, by filling it up."
Their inflamed passions and fiery kisses
spun beyond the bounds of hot caresses.

Reluctant Voyeur

Being judgmental would have been wrong
but their moaning and groaning all night long
stoked memories of Felix. It was disturbing . . .
and aroused feelings Lotte had been curbing.

She could not ignore them as she was lying
directly below them. But she kept trying.
Gloria and Sammy continued passionately
to kiss, caress and moan incessantly.

Lotte felt trapped beneath all this action . . .
an unwitting witness to this raw passion.
Being forced to witness this sizzling act
was akin to being erotically hijacked.

Lotte hoped the bed under their weight
would not collapse and seal her fate.
When finally their passions were abated,
they both sneaked down, quite satiated.

"The lady below slept so soundly."
"Sammy, you performed profoundly."
"I want more, Gloria . . . I'll come tomorrow."
To Lotte this prospect caused further sorrow.

She did not condemn them or even resent,
their physical needs. Her reasons were different.
If she had found Felix, she too would have done it.
In the meantime, she had to focus on his spirit.

Next morning she told David, "It may not be right
that I share a room with Gloria for another night."
David asked her the reason. Lotte replied:
"One woman's secrets another must hide."
"Lotte, regarding Gloria, let me confess,
that I know more than you could even guess.
She lives her life differently . . .
because of her 'free spirit' personality."

"We told you so!" the women began teasing.
Lotte knew God loves each one of His offspring.
"Gloria hurt no one, so I shut my ears.
She need not worry or have any fears.
Her secret was safe from these hypocrites.
Don't in their cupboards skeletons exist?"

Crossroads of Life

Lotte chose hard work to escape the ills
and pressures of life. It helped pay her bills.
Working with her talents, Lotte now could
successfully secure her livelihood.

She tutored pupils all day long,
teaching them that melody and song
are an effective therapy to soothe the heart.
Human spirits soar on the wings of art.

So she coped with the overwhelming awe
of her life's emptiness that nobody saw.
A frugal life helps to propel the best
aspects of our faculties to face life's test.

"If I fail to find Felix, for this reason,
my savings shall help life's leaner season."
She prayed during spells of unbearable pain:
"Please, God, send me back my Felix again."

Do the prayers of the innocent and the weak
victims of life prompt God to speak?
Before everything around collapses,
He intervenes for His vigil never lapses.

A Magician's Secret

A German magician immigrated one day –
Herbert Nivelli arrived in New York to stay.
His Italian sounding name was mysterious and strange.
But his magic tricks brought on a soothing change.

He joined the variety shows as a magician.
Lotte was the group's singer and musician.
Herbert performed with her in many a show.
His past was a paradox. Was he friend or foe?

He avoided questions. One day Herbert
dodged them by transforming a cake into dirt.
Using magic to distract was his habit.
Once from his hat he pulled out a rabbit.
He would display an object then make it flip
or distract his questioners with a magic trick.

Lotte went to dine in the quietest of places
to wistfully observe the passing faces.
Suddenly she got a very big scare . . .
Herbert came over and requested to share
her table with him. Then, he just silently sat
while Lotte was curious and wanted to chat!

"I'll tell you my secret," Herbert declared,
"by your gypsy green eyes I am ensnared.
Without you, my queen, I have an empty life.
I'll be a good husband, if you'll be my wife."

His words were similar, there was a trace
of the spirit of Felix in Herbert's face.
Some ethereal force made her rejoice.
An echo of Felix resounded in Herbert's voice.

Did Felix use Herbert's body as a vehicle?
Herbert was mysterious and Lotte was quizzical.
Can the spirits of living people also travel?
Felix lives somewhere . . . this puzzle must unravel.
Herbert's presence started to ease her tragic hue.
Lotte started seeking him whenever she felt blue.

What was his background? She was on the brink
of asking him, then stopped to think . . .
judging people by their religion is really shallow.
Everyone's individual values mold and follow
their peer pressure and how parents breed
them through childhood. That is the seed.

Web of Destiny

The jukebox started to play very loud.
It drowned the din of the jabbering crowd.
Herbert's mysterious past put her in a trance.
Was her loyalty to Felix floundering, perchance?

To the unfolding events Lotte now began
wondering whether Herbert was the man
chosen (in the interim) until Felix was found.
Were her emotions being stirred on the rebound?

Her swirling senses became complex
and affected her thoughts in a reflex
reaction that caused her great strife.
Her faith in a reunion was very rife.

Herbert put her in a spot extremely grim
by insisting that she must soon marry him.
She replied that for Felix she must wait.
He thought she was unrealistic or obstinate.

Herbert's proposal made her forlorn.
Many other women to him were drawn.
But since she loved Felix, she was not . . .
did reality elude her or was she distraught?

"Herbert, please try to understand me.
Felix made his promises most faithfully.
Don't call me crazy, please, Herbert dear.
As clear as daylight, I feel Felix near.
I would really love to be your wife,
but I belong to Felix, even in afterlife.
Marrying you will be betrayal of his trust.
The pedestal of love may sink into dust.
Suppose I decide to marry you . . .
and Felix comes home and discovers two
husbands in my life. Both nevertheless
marvelous men indeed. To this, I confess."

Lotte did not want to accept being widowed.
"To promises of eternal love this much is owed."
She could not betray Felix. "I would be distraught
if Felix did this, so let's banish the thought."

Did the horrible atrocities, cries and shouts
impair her thoughts? Or were they blackouts?
She heard Felix whisper, "My bonny bride,
the confusion in your mind is bona fide."

Was Lotte loony or perhaps groggy?
Reality is muddled when the mind is foggy.
People are prone, like frogs in a well,
to stay quite smug wherever they dwell.

Fear is a factor beyond a familiar wall.
Herbert's past or religion did not matter at all.
The feminine criteria of a good man
is that he loves and takes care of his woman.

Goodness does not come from being too pious.
Facades of religious zeal perpetuates bias.
"Herbert has a dark side," Lotte's friends opined.
"His character is dubious and past ill-defined.
He may be an escaped Nazi disguised as an Italian."
Everyone offered a different and frightful opinion.

"Maybe he directly or indirectly committed crimes.
Italians were staunch German allies in those times.
For Felix, Lotte, you were uncompromising
so even considering Herbert's proposal is surprising.
What if he was involved in criminal actions?
Why don't you do some discreet investigations?"

The Mystery Deepens

Herbert refused to disclose his religion or past.
He held on to his secrets very steadfast.
He would retort by saying, "This subject is taboo."
Then clam up abruptly – what could Lotte do?

To elicit reciprocity she would narrate her past.
She could feel it pained him. Then he got lost
in some distant memories of his past years.
What dark secret filled his eyes with tears?

Lotte's friends and relatives were full of ire.
"From the frying pan Lotte, you are leaping into fire.
You are desperate because you are lonely.
Look for other men, why Herbert only?
His murky past may well be criminal . . .
or he's hiding something very diabolical.
Your devotion to Felix is sublime and superb.
Do not waste it on this mysterious Herbert!
Your love for Felix is so rare on this earth . . .
don't let such feelings fade in their worth.
If physical needs drive you, they need curbing.
Your emotional equilibrium is quite disturbing."

Herbert's mysterious moods made him reticent.
Lotte's probing made him all the more silent.
Did some monster lurk behind his charm?
Lotte's intuitions found him to be warm.

If people do not want their love to whittle,
they must learn to forgive and overlook a little.
Couples must try to be missing parts of each other.
This happens if they make compromises together.

The warnings of all who were near and dear
were confusing Lotte. She was filled with fear.
"Lotte don't forget how we were victims
of fanatics who propound radical maxims."

Lotte sought more wisdom from those who knew.
"Life is the spectrum of many a different view.
If your conscience is comfortable with the directions
of your chosen path, then ignore the distractions.

Divinity responds differently to each person's prayer.
Maybe Herbert was designated to be your savior.
A flower's thorns or thistles do not discount its worth.
Repentant sinners can be redeemed on earth!"

The Price of Prejudice

Herbert kept insisting that they be married.
Lotte's response continued to remain arid.
He then narrated a story he had heard.
Herbert repeated it for her, word by word . . .

"One man's fanaticism had made him blind.
He hated all the other religions of mankind.
This made him to contemptuously spurn
good people of other faiths at every turn.

'People of other faiths lack credulity.'
He could kill for his religion's purity.
His radical perspectives made him blind.
They colored and prejudiced his narrow mind.

One day floodwaters totally surrounded
this man's house . . . he was quite confounded.
'This problem for us is but a bubble . . .
people of my religion will save me from this trouble.
Take back your boat I'll soon show you proof.'
The rising waters forced him up on the roof.

Yet he continued to boastfully state:
'My people shall come, they may be late.'
The waters rose higher, but the man
climbed higher saying, 'My prayers can
get me God's help that shall soon appear.
We are a sect of winners. I need not fear.

We are God's special people. He delivers
us from our enemies, earthquakes or rivers.
Energy from praying will make waters recede.
We are God's faithful . . . He will fulfill our need.

Should infidels help me? Hell, no way!
You go away, please. Allow me to pray.
Our religion is a weapon with which we attack
all enemies and win. Infidels cannot hack
my faith and belief.' When all logic profound
was rejected by him, the fanatic drowned.

Face to face with God, he indignantly said,
'I prayed so much, then why am I dead?
All the time to You I prayed. Nothing else would I do.
Then is this my reward for praying so much to You?'

God explained: *"The boat people you refused,
are also my children. My creations you abused.
I am the parent of everyone. No one is superior.
I may make them different, but not inferior.*

*You were your own victim. Your medieval rules
inhibit human growth and foster abuse.
A holier-than-thou attitude is degeneracy.
Every divisive preaching is, in fact, a heresy."*

Truth shone from this story, Lotte was certain.
Herbert thus helped her to lift a curtain.
She saw a message emerge like a ray of light.
Enlightened people welcome enhancement of sight.

Sweet Deliverance

Lotte viewed Herbert as God's rescue boat.
A divine deliverance sent to set her afloat.
For drowning people, even a straw will do.
"Tell me, Herbert, did Felix send you?"

To accept Felix's death unhinged her existence.
She was at crossroads but Herbert's persistence
was strangely welcome. He was a cherished friend.
Subconsciously she was glad that he was determined.

"Call me prejudiced or imposing my sermon.
But Herbert is a blue-eyed blond German.
He may have participated in the human sufferings."
Lotte loved Herbert so she ignored such warnings.

She also believed that bodies are interchangeable.
Divine miracles are amazing, so this is also possible.
God can choose to deliver dispensation
by transmigrating spirits to ease deprivation.

Lotte sought answers by fine-tuning that day
her ability to hear the echoes from far away.
The message received from heavens above
was: "Death never ends any true love."

For her this had a special meaning.
"Lotte, have faith in the divine steering
of kindred spirits into what is available.
People bond better if they are compatible."

Her fears evaporated, so without a smudge
she went with Herbert before a city judge.
The judge then declared them man and wife
and wished the couple a happy future life.

Born Lotte Sommer, after marriage she became
Lotte Joseph . . . and now Nivelli, a mysterious name.
Though Herbert's face was bright and beaming
Lotte sensed his heart was silently screaming.

Is Marriage a Panacea?

A husband or wife must not steal
the other's space. They must feel
gratified in giving their loving care
to each other by being a devoted pair.

Deep within them they were well aware
of their need for each other as a pair.
Herbert to her became such an integral part
that she cocooned him deep inside her heart.
They focused on sunsets, rainbows and flowers.
Nature's invaluable wonders filled their hours.

In a mysterious way Lotte began perceiving
Herbert and Felix as a single being.
When Herbert touched her, she very much,
in a sublime way felt her Felix's touch.

Even as she was in Herbert's embrace,
to her it seemed Felix shared the space.
Herbert felt this and told Lotte, "I find
that your responses are of a surreal kind.
I can't help sensing Felix is stealing
your moments with me and you are feeling
his presence . . . and I only remind
you of him. But I really don't mind.
If that makes you happy, my angel dove,
I am glad to be a reflection of Felix's love.
Since you cannot help it, as I can guess,
I'll seek my pleasures in your happiness."

Show business involved them deeper and deeper.
Lotte clung to Herbert like a loving creeper.
So always together that people began to poke
fun at her possessiveness. They began to joke:
"Are you Siamese twins, inseparable all the while?"
Others gazed at them with a quizzical smile.
"You both share such a single-minded path.
We bet you are together even when you take a bath."

Herbert combined comedy with magic to endear
himself to his audience and give them cheer.
His laughter seemed external for deep inside,
Lotte sensed a darkness. What did Herbert hide?

Was Herbert's past very tragic or unpleasant?
Why did it haunt him to damage the present?
Was he trying to hide some very dark memories?
Did he participate in those nightmarish atrocities?

Herbert and Lotte's personal magic took a quantum leap. Their recipe to spiritual stratosphere, if followed faithfully, could uplift many a soul. To the believers no proof is necessary. The skeptics, however, would challenge even well documented facts, condemning them as forgeries.

Compromises in Marriage

They noted that when their shows would commence,
with Lotte's classical songs for a variety show audience,
the level of appreciation was not very rewarding.
Herbert's magic-n-comedy had them applauding.

Lighthearted entertainment they preferred to witness.
Herbert's magic and comedy fell in the fitness
of these people's expectations. The shows had to adapt.
Lotte understood and agreed to change her act.

When Herbert's magic and conjuring feat
were given more importance – it was a treat.
The sponsors were also of the same mind.
They told Lotte, "You are considerate and kind."

The sacrifice was not easy, for she had spent long
years and hard work to master classical song.
Since many children attended, Lotte could sense
Herbert's magic would better regale the audience.

Even if that were not so, Lotte was alert
to her husband's needs and was not hurt.
She always agreed to compromise and despite
her own needs, she did what was right.

Lotte became his assistant on the stage
to help Herbert become a greater rage.
Soon several sponsors now invited
them to perform. They were excited.

Lotte beams at "Twinkle" who stole the limelight with his cute bird-antics during the Nivelli magic shows.

The Nevillis as a team gained a new dimension.
The children drew Herbert's special attention.
He was so happy when they laughed with joy.
Herbert would behave just like a little boy.

Excitement of showbiz helps temporarily
to soothe the pains of the sad and lonely.
Yet pain can persist without repose.
People's masks hide more than what shows.

Something with Herbert seemed not all right.
His silent tears flowed secretly every night.
Many a morning Lotte noticed his pillow was wet.
What events of the past was he fighting to forget?

She had agreed not to probe . . . for that reason only
she would broach the subject by talking of her lonely
life and reasons for why she was driven
away from Germany. Herbert remained sullen.

He immersed himself in work for their sake.
It was also therapeutic. He wanted to make
a home where peace for both would prevail.
When their bodies creaked, their spirits could sail.

Beyond physical frontiers through fancy flights,
we can discover vistas of surreal sights.
To the past and present each spouse must adjust.
Without compromises, a marriage can bust.

Herbert's Secret Revealed

One night in his sleep Herbert started screaming.
He was shivering and shaking while he was dreaming.
In his sleep he was shouting, "No, please, I beg you."
Lotte felt helpless, not knowing what to do.

In her loving arms, she began to cradle him.
What kind of nightmare could be so grim?
Like a frightened child, in the arms of his mother
Herbert was whimpering and began to sputter . . .

He was *not* Herbert Nivelli but Herbert Lewin.
Born a German Jew and educated in Berlin.
Like all German citizens he was attached
to his fatherland, with a loyalty unmatched.

Young Herbert Lewin performed magic tricks
since childhood with cards, stones and sticks.
He spread happiness and soon became
at a very early age, a famous name.

He grew to be a handsome young man,
and wanting to succeed, diligently began
cultivating his skills. He saved enough pelf
to buy the best books and educate himself.

He progressed fast. People found it strange
to see such a young man play the stock exchange.
Herbert surfed the market's rise and fall
and with great aplomb . . . he stood tall!

He lived with fellow Germans in peace and amity
when subterfuge for survival became a necessity.
The family went to such lengths, you'll be surprised
that despite being Jewish, he was not circumcised.

The Berliners loved and respected the Lewins.
They were honorable people of noble means.
But an ominous cloud and an inimical air
began terrorizing everybody, everywhere.
The Nazi juggernaut unleashed its calamities.
Doom engulfed the German-Jewish families.

Even remote traces of Jewish lineage made
people prime targets . . . everyone was afraid.
As a German, he hoped this crisis would pass.
But mass hysteria fanned the flames – alas!

Hitler's haranguing and villainous sermons
made Germans rabid against Jewish Germans.
Herbert saw beyond the theatrics and realized
he must escape before worse crimes were organized.
Horrendous Nazi propaganda was becoming a curse
and was creating for Jews, a collective hearse.

It became climactic when Hitler's S.S. one day
raided the stock exchange and marched Herbert away.
All Jewish traders were stripped of their claims.
They became candidates for the Nazi flames.

Herbert's brother-in-law, Rudolph Freund, posed for this keepsake photograph in front of the magic paraphernalia store "Hokus Pokus", in Prague, Czechoslovakia. The Nazis subsequently shut the store and interned Herbert and his family.

Blood-soaked blossoms in Berlin then bloomed.
Herbert planned his escape before he was doomed.
He had to make haste in order to save
himself from the spreading Nazi hate-wave.

He took his fiancée, Gerda, in a car
along with his mother safe and far.
When he reached Czechoslovakia's border,
the guards stopped him to enforce the Nazi order.

"Why are you leaving? Are you returning soon?"
Herbert pulled out a hen as a magical boon.
Presenting it to the guards, he said, "At least
I want you to enjoy a chicken feast!"

The guards were amused: "Is that so?
Well then, dear magician, we'll let you go."
Herbert settled in Prague and without delay
rented a modest store to earn his way.

He named this small store *Hokus Pokus.*
Passersby murmured, "It's only to provoke us
that he chose this name. He is daft."
In showmanship, Herbert had great craft.

He found unique ways to promote his curios.
He sold them with magic tricks laid out in rows.
To tempt passersby he would place an easy pick,
outside as enticement, for them to grab quick.

Whoever tried failed, for the curio in a trice
zipped back into the store to claim its price.
Those who followed it were eager to seek
explanations about this novel technique.

The people thus 'tricked' to enter his store
exclaimed they never saw such gimmicks before!
They became customers for other very nice
curios from *Hokus Pokus* for a good price.

His terms were reasonable . . . rather cheap!
Veritable bargains for his customers to keep.
His goodwill spread and Herbert soon became
a successful tradesman of enviable fame.

Hard work and ingenuity made him prosperous.
He was very humble and delightfully humorous.
A happy transformation then happened in his life . . .
his fiancée, Gerda, agreed to be his wife.

A Son is Born

In September, 1937, a sweet baby boy
was born – Peter became their greatest joy!
Gerda was happy that she could bear
for Herbert a beloved son and heir.

Herbert looked towards heaven with grateful eyes
and exclaimed, "O greatest Magician in the skies,
our mortal magic tricks are infinitely puerile
compared to the miracle of a baby's smile.
Peter's smile is brighter than a million earthlights.
We are blessed to be granted your gift that delights.
Gerda and I are grateful and also very honored
to nurture your creation so priceless and hallowed."

Peter was a cute boy growing every moment.
The glimmer of divinity in him was evident.
To protect his son, Herbert twisted the name Lewin.
He made it Nivelli hoping that this would stave off ruin.

Hoping to fool Jew-hunters, Herbert felt great.
But could he have likewise, twisted his fate?
Herbert's efforts failed when German troops
invaded Czechoslovakia in sudden swoops.

All the Jews were arrested. The Nivelli family
despite their new name suffered calamity.
They were taken to Auschwitz. All hell broke loose.
Herbert had hoped the Nivellis would escape this noose.

He was separated from his mother, wife and son.
For the Nivellis, the holocaust had earnestly begun.
He survived by entertaining his camp guards.
Performing magic tricks with sodden playing cards.

He entertained them hoping that they may kindly
reciprocate by treating his family humanely.
He knew in Auschwitz most inmates were doomed.
His family must survive the fate that loomed.

The Nazis wondered how his magic was done.
Herbert performed to save his mother, wife and son.
Their fate, without his efforts, carried bleak odds.
Herbert tried to improve it by entertaining these clods.

"Your family shall receive our special grace.
We'll reward you by putting them in a fine place."
The Nazi promises, heaven knew well,
were made on earth but fulfilled in hell.

"Herbert, your magic is really great.
We promise to change your family's fate.
They shall not suffer the fate of those
who our Fuhrer considers Germany's foes."

He had no option but to believe these liars.
Would his family be safe from their fires?
No one with a conscience can tell such lies.
Herbert worked harder to save their lives.

Herbert hoped and prayed that his little son Peter was in the loving arms of his mother, Gerda Nivelli (as seen above) when the Nazi gas chambers snuffed their lives.

Murder Most Foul

One day, as he performed and they were being thrilled,
at about the same time . . . his family was being killed.
As the fires were consuming his mother, wife and son
the Nazis cheered his magic, exclaiming, "What fun!"

Each beloved member was murdered during or after
Herbert's magic shows. Perhaps the Nazi laughter
had blended with their shrieks. A tragedy grotesque
was inflicted on Herbert by his cheering audience.

"We have God's power," the fiends boasted.
They killed his only child and cruelly roasted
his young wife and old mother, even while,
Herbert performed for them with a smile.

After liberation Herbert sadly set his sights,
only on searching through days and nights
for his loved ones. Starving and in pain,
Herbert was relentless like someone insane.

Like a madman, he wandered here and there.
His fading hopes made him tear his hair.
Herbert beat his chest as he climbed the rungs
of hysteria's ladder. He screamed off his lungs.

They had made a list, these demon-brained.
His family was included among the bloodstained
in this camp that the world despised and hated.
Herbert wished he was dead and not liberated.

What rationale or motives can be blamed
for these acts? Were they demons or deranged?
Herbert would never hold his son again.
The despair that ensued would not wane.

Sapped by the agony of being left alone,
his legs crumpled . . . no longer his own.
He crawled in a stupor and hardly slept.
He would scream at every one he met:
"They have killed my son . . . did you know?
Also my wife and mother, so I must follow
to meet them on the other side."
Herbert was determined to commit suicide.

He climbed and leapt from a height.
He wanted to end his lonely plight.
People prayed, "Please, kind God, at length,
restore this poor man's sanity and strength."

Maybe with their prayers, death hid like a fugitive.
Some divine plan decided that Herbert must live.
Destiny directed his migration to New York.
Herbert dealt with his past by refusing to talk.

A Spiritual Son

Peter became Lotte's spiritual son from that time.
His absence was a presence, sweet and sublime.
Peter helped Herbert and Lotte to laugh
by beaming at them from his photograph.

He became tangible and did not withdraw.
He glimmered in faces of other lads they saw.
Lotte bonded with him through the echoes of love
which Peter transmitted from Heavens above.

She heard his voice . . . it could not be sweeter
for it echoed the spiritual love of Peter.
"My beloved new mother, they failed to burn
my love for father. I shall spiritually return."

To Lotte, Peter's words of love were soothing.
In absence of a body the spirit is a-blooming.
Divine dynamics reveal spectrums that can
stoke our eternity . . . this is the grand plan.

Lotte wanted a son so Herbert could embrace
the spirit of his Peter, in their child's face.
She tried to become pregnant, but sadly could not
despite medical help. This put her in a spot.

She could have had children, lovely little scamps,
had her body not been damaged in Nazi camps.
The gift of motherhood is natural, not rare . . .
but harmful events destroy it beyond repair.

This inner emotion, so supremely human
is stronger than ocean waves in most women.
A yearning that her womb should help to multiply,
is an instinct which nature wants to glorify.

In every bird, deer, lioness or hare,
the ache for motherhood is everywhere.
Fulfillment can also come through adoptions.
Eternal blessings blossom with spiritual connections.

Sublimating Yearnings

Doctors told Lotte that she would never conceive.
Would Herbert's dreams end? Would he grieve?
"If you cannot give me a son, Lotte, let me reassure
you that my love shall continue for it is very pure.
I'll love you, Lotte, through sunshine or rain.
Love means sharing disappointments and pain.
Whenever I miss Peter, I'll stage a children's show,
their laughter and mirth shall make me aglow."

Herbert layered dimensions to his magic wand
by his feelings for children that went beyond
the comprehension of many. Among all in the hall,
Herbert's focus was on children, big and small.

Often Herbert mysteriously smiled
with love-lit eyes at a particular child.
He was invoking Peter's spirit with the spell
of his magical abilities . . . Lotte could tell.

That child would begin to bear in his face
the traces of the soft and charming grace
of their beloved Peter, who, right from the start
and after his death, lived on in Herbert's heart.

Herbert sought Peter's presence everywhere.
In children of all ages . . . in their eyes and hair.
In every boy he would seek (sad or pleasant),
memories of Peter, which were ever present.

SPORTS, RADIO, FEATURES
THURSDAY, SEPTEMBER 29, 1949

Magicians Plan Convention Here

A man whose life was spared because he knew magic will highlight the 13th annual New England convention of magicians in Worcester next month at The Sheraton Hotel.

Bay State Magic Club, Ring 33, International Brotherhood of Magicians, will be host. Five hundred delegates are expected Oct. 21, 22 and 23. This is the first time in 11 years the convention will be in this city.

Herbert Nivelli of Forest Hills, N. Y., who will perform, has been in this country two years. He came from Germany where he spent four years in four different concentration camps. He lost his parents, wife and child in the gas chambers of Auschwitz. The Nazis at the camp did not execute him because he entertained them every night with feats of magic.

Registration and a Nite Before

HERBERT NIVELLI
Magician Here Next Month

Newspaper clipping from 1949 documents how magic enabled Herbert to escape execution. Unfortunately, he could not save his mother, wife and child from the gas chambers of Auschwitz.

Herbert had a repertoire of forty-six
clever and entertaining conjuring tricks.
He poured out his feelings as he performed.
People's hearts would be regaled and warmed.

To excite children he would make a painted ball
float over their heads and all around the hall.
He would produce a chicken from his cap
and make the children laugh and clap.

He would pull colored ribbons from his sleeves,
then convert them magically into leaves.
Balloons became oranges, which sprightly waiters
distributed after the shows to his little spectators.

Like many comedians, Herbert suppressed
the acute pains lingering deep in his breast.
Without a shred of humanity the Nazis had cast
his beloved son Peter in their genocidal blast.

Lotte and Herbert's laughter and silent tears,
their pains, pleasures, the past and present fears,
would cast dark clouds. But then, the sunshine
of a commitment to love made life sublime.

By the frustration for what distinctly remained
Herbert's unfulfilled wish, Lotte was pained.
Her reproductive abilities were not healing.
Motherhood to her represented a feeling.

The doctors kept trying. Herbert must not lose
his hopes for a son. He did not accuse
Lotte for failing. He was graceful and gentle.
His spiritual consciousness molded his mettle.

This expanded their visions of a dream world
where for all humanity, a banner is unfurled . . .
under which all aspiring fathers or mothers
can lovingly care for the children of others.

Ideaology Divides Korea

The Koreans began fighting during that time,
over different ideologies . . . *another* senseless crime!
The Korean War made life very dreary.
All those involved were pained and weary.
Lotte and Herbert went to Korea to entertain
and witnessed Koreans destroying each other in vain.

As a magician's helper Lotte ably assisted
him in his shows. Some people persisted
in asking question after irrational question.
"Sir, is your magic not a marginal dimension
of your greater capabilities? So, please save my life,
by making my wife become another man's wife!"

Another asked, "Dear magician, I shall revere
your magic if you can make lust disappear!
Lust spawns evil, making cannon fodder
of fellow humans, who are someone's son or daughter.

Lotte was inexplicably gravitating to the two young Indian Sikhs serving in Korea, during 1950, under the U.N. flag. Was fate's mysterious plan in the process of unfolding?

First Sikh Encounter

One day their magic show was very taxing.
Two fresh voices perked it up by asking
strange questions, the kind Herbert had never
heard before. Full of meaning and clever!
The two Sikh youths' earnestness filled the air.
They were young and a very handsome pair.

"Sat Sri Akaal, Sir! God is the only truth."
The Nivellis were thus greeted by the sikh youth.
"Since you are a magician, it seems very clear
you can make things appear and disappear.
Then mighty magician why don't you banish
hatred from earth so that warfare would vanish?
Extinguish ill feelings and make the call
to end every war and bring peace to all."

What Lotte detected, in Herbert's smile,
was a mild amusement devoid of guile.
He was great at repartees. Lotte was in awe.
Both had never ever seen Sikhs before.
This pair had come to meet their obligations
in the peacekeeping forces of the United Nations.

"Your answer is being ready, please peer at
what I shall pull out of my conjuror's hat.
Hear my magic words that shall go beyond
conventional comprehension. Watch my wand.
'Aabra ka Dabra', please work magic powers."
Herbert then pulled out a bunch of flowers.

He divided the flowers equally into two.
"You take this one, and this one is for you.
Different colors, shapes, smells – how odd!
Yet each creation is a wonder of God.
Short spells of success do not crown a mortal fate
or give the arrogant a right to dispense hate.
By banishing barriers, problems are resolved.
Humility helps humanity to be better evolved.
God had a purpose in creating diversity.
For being different, no one deserves hostility.
A universal brotherhood propels human hope."
Lotte strongly subscribed to this vision's scope.

Herbert staged magic shows, again and again.
Traveling to different towns on a military plane.
One flight in particular had them very ruffled.
With bad weather, they were tossed and shuffled.

Besides entertainers, the plane had been loaded
with ammonia gas bottles . . . one of them exploded!
It filled the plane with a choking smell,
creating a nauseating, suffocating hell.

Everyone thought that the plane would explode
and transport its passengers into death's abode.
But the experienced pilot, with his deft hands,
managed to land the plane on solid lands.

High Sea Drama

Once on a merry cruise they booked their show.
The rough sea heaved with its ebb and flow.
Herbert with his magic regaled the audience.
His hope for a son became their life's essence.

Herbert's German accent was very pronounced.
To overcome this handicap, in jest he announced,
"I'm a professor of broken English." He thought it fit
to spice and spike his performance with wit.

A stupid passenger stated, "It's a great cruise,
because on it I find there are no Jews . . .
with them the ship would have been tainted."
Lotte heard him and she nearly fainted.

Herbert and Lotte felt like they were grabbed
by the racially prejudiced, and verbally stabbed.
"Pity him," Herbert said as he read her expression.
While he consoled her, he fought his own depression.

"Forget it," Herbert added. "It should not affect us.
People's mental aberrations make them lose focus.
Too many drinks have made him a punk.
Beasts behave better than a bigot who is drunk.
This world bears fools and the bigoted galore.
We have two options – forgive them or ignore!
For his own good, I am tempted to go and tell
him where his kind thrive – it is deep in hell."

Herbert embraced Lotte and snuggled close.
By forgiving the bigot, they both chose
to expunge the hurt he stirred that day.
They were triumphant by casting anger away.

Shallow people project the façade of superior worth.
Those with genuine merit tread humbly on earth.
Each person is to someone loved and cherished.
By disparaging God's creations, many have perished.

When people are assaulted with words or guns,
that pain is suffered by God's daughters and sons.
Are parents not pained by their child's abuse?
The pain God suffers is far more profuse.

Waning Wanderlust

Herbert and Lotte both could not ignore
their advancing age. Their energy no more
could cope with their schedules. Now their desire
was to curtail their assignments and quietly retire.

They sought a place for a peaceful repose,
away from the hectic pace of the shows.
Like two happy children with one single thought,
when they found what they wanted, it was bought.

It was a cute little cottage in the countryside.
Together in peace, here they hoped to reside.
Greater than the external, the world within,
deep in ourselves, is the one to win.

Shifting Sands of Time

Doctors detected a fault in Herbert's heartbeat.
Was his stress level high or did he overeat?
Diets deemed healthy many years ago
were debunked by doctors who said: "It's not so!"

Medical research found that fat and internal heat
had adverse effects on the human heartbeat.
Herbert's eating habits had to be tempered.
Health suffers if taste buds are pampered.

Old couples in love often find one another
in altered roles. Herbert acted like a father.
Lotte, in turn, cared for him like a mother.
Many couples behave like parents to each other.
Each ready and willing to sacrifice one's all
for the other's sake. They respond to the call
of the mutual love they have been sharing.
Such interdependence is part of pairing.

But some sad day (who can foretell?),
death inevitably steals one from a life so parallel.
The plight of the lonely one left behind, indeed,
causes great grief and creates a special need.
Whoever knew Lotte and Herbert always swore
that they had never seen so much love before.

Lotte did her best to keep his body trim
but Herbert loved to eat – a compulsion with him.
Eating helped him alleviate his sad mood.
He submerged those feelings with comfort food.

Herbert changed very much in 1977.
He communicated incessantly with Peter in heaven.
"Peter's voice is clearer," he began to cogitate
about the Nivelli legacy. "What shall be its fate?"

Life without a son became a sterile routine.
Herbert's pain was deep, although unseen.
Days would pass, but fan an inner flame.
He feared for the future of the Nivelli name . . .
"Will its significance fade when I am gone?"
He had coined it, so he was forlorn.

On the radio a somber song began to play.
Its lyrics made Herbert melancholy all day.
"Aft we ascend, shall we meet again?"
The depth of meaning and the mournful strain
of the singer's voice, cut deep like a knife.
He asked, "Is there another life after this life?"

His moods drifted from despair to hope.
Between the present and Peter, how did he cope?
I hate to leave but I hear Peter beckoning:
"Daddy I miss you . . . when are you coming?"

All our attachments related to this earth
are not the reason for which we took birth.
After playing our part, we must accept the fact
of others taking over . . . nothing remains intact.

On earth, the duration of this life spans
barely a billionth fraction of our cosmic dance.
We must move on graciously and not scar the soul
by hanging on so desperately that it exacts a toll.

Whatever in this life that we have sown
shall be what we reap. Our soul has grown
proportionately here to whatever we plant.
The glories of a good deed are greater than a chant.

Doom at the Doorsteps

At their lawyer's office Herbert choked for breath.
His face grew pale with fast approaching death.
He was sweating profusely in unbearable pain.
Lotte's panic was pathetic and difficult to contain.

She was screaming at her wretched fate.
Help in an emergency always seems late.
"If the delay is any longer, it will make no sense."
At last, she heard the sirens of an ambulance.

His own peril Herbert was hardly heeding,
as he turned to Lotte and started pleading:
"The Nivelli name . . . remember that it represents
religious tolerance to promote secular ends.
Lewin becoming Nivelli tells the story
of my struggles against the sordid pillory
religious extremists inflict upon mankind.
Let this name lend lofty visions to the blind."

Then Herbert died. Lotte cried to God and said,
"Instead of Herbert I wish I were dead.
If this is your wish, God, then let me only live
to fulfill his dreams. This is my life's motive."

Then Lotte became numb, stunned by it all.
No more entertainment in the hall.
No more laughter, no more song.
No more magic – it all turned wrong!
She was lost, lonely and woe be-gone.
How did she muster her will to live on?

Herbert's love echoed: "Only my body died,
my soul shall serve you from the other side.
Leaving you alone makes me feel very guilty,
but God knows that women have the ability
to manage crisis better. Most men are weak.
True strength is not measured by the physique."

The Loneliest Feeling

Lotte returned home and trembled on her knees.
Without Herbert, she fumbled with her keys.
When the front door opened to an empty room,
sad reality engulfed her like a fog of gloom.

The house felt eerie and unusually damp -
like being back in the concentration camp.
Her first moments without Herbert seemed to be
painfully torturous. She could hardly hear or see.

Fond memories floated as she stood alone.
She pined for Herbert who was her very own.
Friends and acquaintances came to console
but their measured sympathies seared her soul.

Sometimes formal gestures aggravate the grief.
They reopen the wounds in need of relief.
With probing questions, her anguish grew worse.
She yearned for solitude and hoped they'd disperse.

When the visitors left, she quickly shut the door.
She turned around and felt a painful sore.
A wound began to fester in her empty heart.
What should she do? Where could she start?

Her tear-filled eyes examined her circumstances.
Denial can soothe only in some instances.
To cope, she repudiated a death once more.
She went into the kitchen as she did before.

"Herbert, come down and sit with me.
I have your piping hot cup of coffee.
Just like you enjoy it, nice and strong.
You've been in the bathroom a bit too long.
Your coffee on the table is getting cold.
Come and drink it . . . put your bathing on hold.
Two cups are waiting as they always do,
one for me and the other one for you."

Dreams, Denial and Reality

Can dreams be fulfilled after a person dies?
Love continues to radiate from the skies.
Edith visited Lotte to reaffirm deathlessness.
She spread the board to play virtual chess.
The sisters played with checkered pawns.
Edith was alive in Lotte's dusks and dawns.

Dreams engineer and mould our lives for sure.
Lotte always felt being in the company of four.
"God, please bear witness from your azure sky.
We are all together. Herbert, Felix, Peter and I."

Her marriage to Felix had lasted just
ten years. Then his body was turned to dust.
She conquered death many times in Auschwitz,
before Herbert breezed in with his showbiz and glitz.
The Gypsy's prediction of forty years came to play,
counting thirty years as Mrs. Nivelli, in the U.S.A.

During their thirty years of married life,
Herbert was a loving husband and she, a loyal wife.
In Herbert, the conjuror, Lotte had begun
to feel glimmers of Felix. Her love had won!
"Ten years with Felix and thirty in marriage
to Herbert were a blessing and a privilege.
Dear Gypsy, your forty years prediction was true.
But what about the son that was foretold by you?
I hope that was not just a tale you had spun.
Herbert needs a son and I promised him one."

Travel as Therapy

Her relatives in Milwaukee wrote her a letter,
"Dear Lotte, we think that you had better,
come here for a break away from your pain.
We love you and want you to quickly enplane.
Herbert was both your husband and lover.
From a loss so severe, we'll help you recover.
Loneliness after a thirty-year companionship
can be very painful, so please take this trip.
Herbert is not going to return from his grave.
In the face of adversities you were always brave.
This change will help. Please come, we await
to see you, we hope, at a very early date."

Lotte accepted their invitation. The flight was rough.
Dark clouds and gnashing winds made it tough.
Most passengers in the plane began to pray
and wished they had flown on another day.

Soon it became calmer and even the sun
began to shine. Breakfast had begun.
The flight attendants started serving food.
Lotte sank into a melancholy mood.

She saw a deeper meaning in the adjoining seat.
Why was it vacant? Lotte could not eat . . .
the seat seemed as empty as her lonely life.
She imagined Herbert on it to soothe her strife.
Her imaginations helped to ease her stress.
Herbert smiled at her to heal her loneliness.

Hans was born in Germany but had to flee because he was a Jew. His mother, Karla, had died of cancer and his father, Karl Liebmann, died during World War II of loneliness, torture and starvation. Hans' wife, Gerda, had just recently passed away when he met Lotte. The basis of their instant bond was their common circumstances, language and culture.

Echoes of Love

Her ears tuned in and she could hear
Herbert's familiar loving voice, "Lotte dear,
cheer up and smile, this plane is clearly
better than the ammonia gas one, surely
it shall transport you to your relatives who
are kind enough to be waiting for you."

Otto and his wife, Ela, took her for walks.
They did their best with affectionate talks.
They took her to shopping centers and cafes.
A welcome change for Lotte in many ways.

When they were together as a group of three,
Lotte counted four, her Herbert they could not see.
Returning to New York, she soon met perchance,
John Liebmann, whom she lovingly called Hans.

Spirituality versus Scepticism

Hans was a widower who did not bend
to Lotte's beliefs . . . but he became her friend.
He spoke German fluently without a slip.
Both bonded beyond mere companionship.

Lotte was spiritually focused and would plead
that he respect her beliefs. Hans decreed
that she stop being a fool. "I seek the tangible
for they are more believable than the invisible."

Hans' wife, Gerda, died of cancer and left earth
beyond her mortal pains for a heavenly birth.
In spiritual terms Lotte sincerely felt
each one's spouse with them also dwelt.

"Not physically, Hans, but from heavens above,
your wife and my husband continue their love.
They put us together so the physical dimension
of our life suffers less deprivation and tension.

Their spirits were guiding forces for our connections.
Physical entities are driven by spiritual directions.
Lovers never abandon loved ones to grieve.
Directly or indirectly, they arrange a reprieve.

Their roving spirits transcend terrestrial fences
to partake in our lives. Superseding known senses
they facilitate our ability to sprout spiritual wings.
Flying on them liberates us from mundane things.

Spirits of the departed travel through the ether.
They follow loved ones, soft as a feather.
Their presence is strengthened by our memories.
Have faith, Hans, and your pains shall cease.

Isolate your focus to feel your wife around.
She can travel to you, although heaven-bound.
Through spiritual visions you can see them wait
to welcome you . . . at heaven's glorious gate."

"Lotte, this is all hocus-pocus or voodoo.
It suits idle people with nothing else to do.
I don't hear echoes or any heavenly sound.
Nor do I get promptings from spirits around.
The only sound I would like to hear,
is the sound of money. That is a very dear,
sweet music to my ears. Magic and spirituality
for you maybe right. For me it is . . . stupidity."

"Hans, we are actors in earth's sprawling theatre.
Our souls wear bodies gifted by our Creator.
We come to this world curious and impressionable . . .
pliable like clay and so very vulnerable.

As innocent babies to this world we were sent
to learn pertinent lessons from this environment.
A brother, sister, father, friend or mother
each impart their influence as a surrogate tutor.

We play our parts, fulfill this world's obligations,
then depart as scheduled for our final migrations.
Bereft of the earthly baggage we own
our bonds thrive, if we have spiritually grown.

What is life-after-death, Hans, if you ask.
What it was before birth . . . a mysterious mask!
Our understanding is constrained by our sensory zone.
What lies beyond was designed to remain unknown.

With our Creator's plans we must be content.
This short visit and the interactions were meant
to be a growth process during our visit this time.
Proper utilization makes our spirits more sublime.

Life's road maps can lead us to lofty pathways
or trip those who ignore lessons history displays.
Every radical's holier-than-thou pride
is a cover-up for their deceitful short ride.

With wealth our soul's scars shall not ameliorate.
All might and glamour do ultimately deteriorate.
The body atrophies whilst running its course.
The strength of our spirit is a perennial resource.

Acts of love help the human brain
to create memories that can soothe our pain.
Prayers disguised as bargains, heaven will not hear.
But a selfless lover's appeal shall reach God's ear.

To illumine our roadways for an eternal future,
a self-centered attitude we must not harbor.
Clearing our lives of clutter and material love
will open our hearts to the echoes from above.

Gaze with spiritual eyes . . . you'll find through them
God's splendid tapestry and garment's hem.
All the splendors of our eternal tomorrows
can overcome this world's transient sorrows."

Ethereal Echoes

Lotte's cherished memories of childhood days
led her to reminisce on Edith's loving gaze.
Her spiritual connection was forever secure.
Love between sisters shall always endure.

When Lotte needed Edith, her voice would chime
to diminish her despair each and every time.
Sisters in heaven can also be an anchor.
Edith would visit and be her mentor.

"My baby sister, Lotte, are you there?
Let's share a springtime that fills the air.
Lotte, let us play as we always did before
and celebrate our eternal sisterly rapport."

Sisters are mothers in moments that are low.
When siblings share love, their bonds do grow.
Edith's echoes of love, whilst Lotte would sleep,
paved paths of love, subliminal, eternal and deep.

Felix floated in her dreams constantly singing
their favorite song. In her ears kept ringing
the echoes of his voice. It sprouted the wings
of cherished memories and romance of springs.

The medium of music keeps souls attached.
The powers of melody have an effect unmatched.
Attachment and detachment are flip sides indeed.
Our spirits have desires like the body's need.

Detours of Destiny

For Lotte and Hans their mutual needs continued
to bind them . . . a very close relationship ensued.
These needs made them share everything together.
They both suitably complemented each other.

Hans would advise, help and afford
his expertise, be it business or in court.
Real estate, income or taxes of estate,
in all these matters Hans' skills were great.

He took control and his decisions were final.
Lotte and Hans without formal or conventional
rituals of marriage lived as a common law couple.
By pooling resources their strengths did double.

They wanted to sell their house in Groton Street.
It needed repairs; the work was incomplete.
The roof was leaking and the paint on the walls
needed a re-coating in all the rooms and halls.

After the workers left, Lotte heard someone pause
outside the house. Hans was absent for he was
away in his car for an appointment at four.
Lotte said, "Come in," after I knocked on her door.

Lotte Narrates our First Encounter

"Hans, Mickey was humble with a gentle grace.
An inexplicable glow reflected from his face.
He sounded genuine, his presence was great . . .
An ex-moviemaker who branched into real estate.

He displayed expertise in everything . . .
renting, renovating, buying or even clinching
the best deals possible. Hans, he really appeared
dependable and he donned a French-cut beard.

His graying hair exuded a certain image.
He looked dignified and much older than his age.
His clothes were simple, his manners clean.
Hans, he reflected a mystic sheen.
It stirred my spirits mysteriously, I admit.
He had palpable warmth . . . I could almost touch it.
When he offered to give me a ride back home
I declined, but my thoughts began to roam.

I told him to phone you, then I took the bus.
He had business proposals he wished to discuss.
Hans, do discuss and consider his offer.
Examine the merit and decide what is proper."

Spiritual Anchors

Something strange happened as Lotte slept.
Herbert whispered to her as he stealthily crept
between Hans and her. "Lotte, I have made
a plan that on earth shall further my crusade.

It shall unfold slowly and bring back your smile.
Your spirit shall sparkle but Hans may get hostile.
He is not yet enlightened so you cannot blame
him for lacking visions, beyond his current frame.

The responsibility of mine that you shoulder
is becoming more urgent as you get older.
Old age has its needs . . . Hans is many years
older than you are, so I do have fears.

Old age can be very painful and stressful.
Lotte, I earnestly want to see you successful.
God is helping me and has blessed your soul
for you to attain your patiently pursued goal.
With your achievements you shall serve the tormented
and the helpless innocents, victimized by the demented."

Lotte's mind by this dream became enlivened.
Memories and commitments were further ripened.
So she started hoping that one day Hans sees
the splendor that emanates from spiritual entities.
Whenever she would hold or kiss Peter's photograph
Hans ridiculed her hopes with a cynical laugh.

"Lotte, your faith is a wild-goose chase.
Your afterlife mantras ruin my days."
"Hans, please understand that my life is stale.
Without pursuing my promise, my existence is pale."

He remained insensitive and was so unaware
of her commitment to Herbert. "Hans, I can't bear
to fail in my mission. How can I ever
retreat from a pathway we all should discover?"

Hans' obdurate disbelief did always somehow
cause a band of sweat to bead her brow.
He was good at heart but never understood
Lotte's deep felt need to attain motherhood.

Without his knowledge, she had already begun
to secretly and earnestly search for a son.
Hans thought her pursuits were on a nebulous track.
But in spirit she was determined to bring Peter back.

Proper Prioritizing

Hans approved the deal and accepted the rent.
With my proposal Hans was very content.
The deal for some time worked very well.
Then trouble brewed. Hans began to yell . . .

He flew into a rage. Lotte clenched her teeth.
His temper made her nervous, she could not breathe.
Hans then phoned me in deep distress.
"Mickey, your client has created a mess!"

Hans continued to fume and to frown.
Panic-stricken, I paced up and down.
To resolve the problem, I became totally involved.
With my unflinching help, the problem was solved.

Managing properties involves work and expertise.
Hans thought it would be better and wise
to sell the properties . . . each and every one.
I helped them once again and had this done.

The Gravitation

"From all the other agents that we had met,
we trusted Mickey. We did not forget
that he had been instrumental in resolving
our earlier problems . . . a bond was evolving.

He handled each crisis as if it was his.
Hans and I benefited from his expertise.
Of all the other dealers we had tried,
Mickey excelled and Hans was satisfied.

Dr. Stein declared I must be hospitalized.
My polyps were operated. After that I realized
I was very weak, feverish and dizzy.
To help me, the staff became very busy.

Through my ordeal everyone did the best they could.
But a visit from Mickey, I felt, would do me good.
My wish was fulfilled and it brightened my day.
Mickey brought joy with his gift of a bouquet.

On his 'get-well-soon' card was a signature:
Mickey Harbance Kumar. But for me a better
way to sign the card, I wished he had instead
inscribed, 'your son'. . .the one I never had.

Was I foolishly hoping he'd proclaim some day,
'You have found your son. I am here to stay.'
One day, in his presence, I got a form
the hospital needed me to fill as per norm.
With a deep-set sadness churning within
I skipped the blank space against – 'Your next of kin.'

Mickey observed, 'Lotte, please forgive
me for being a little inquisitive. . . .
but why have you not completed that column?'
My desire for a son then made him very solemn.
'Mickey, please can you visit me every day
while I am in this hospital . . . is there a way?'

He started visiting and I began to relate
the turns and twists of my life and fate.
He shared the sad events of his own.
With him I never felt empty and alone.

Hans was impatient with my tales of woe.
Mickey was sympathetic and did not show
ridicule or skepticism like Hans did with me.
People in pain always welcome sympathy.

A past pain echoed with Mickey as I spoke
of Peter's cruel death. He heard that and broke
into a stream of tears that rolled and rolled
spontaneous, profuse and uncontrolled.

Did I unpeel a wound or inadvertently tread
on past pains? I cried too. Then Mickey said,
'Death stamps its indelible mark on each one.
My father died of religious strife like Herbert's son.' "

Celestial Coincidence

"When were you born? 'September 23, 1937.'
I looked up in wonderment towards Heaven.
That year, month and date was also Peter's birthday.
Did Herbert's 'visit' allude to this plan underway?

This coincidence put my emotions into high drive.
Peter would be Mickey's age had he been alive!
In Auschwitz, his infant body was sadly consumed.
Could it be, in another person, his spirit had returned?

When I told Hans why my affinity grew,
he mocked and scorned my point-of-view.
'It's a mere coincidence. Your obsession is playing
tricks on you. Lotte, your mind is straying.'

Was I bleary when Felix, Edith, Herbert, Peter,
my father or mother became a regular visitor?
People who have loved never cease loving.
In some form or level they keep re-connecting.

To help those left behind, loved ones complete
by known or unknown means, an antagonist's defeat.
Against the mightiest foe, spirituality cannot fall.
Could Hans comprehend this concept at all?

He is intelligent but in this sphere, a detractor.
I wish enlightenment helps him fathom this factor.
'The dead cannot communicate, Lotte, this is true.
Please be realistic. I am worried about you.'

Was it mere coincidence that destiny chose to sever
Mickey's father from him and Herbert's son forever?
A father and son whose pained hearts for years
chose the glitz of showbiz to hide their tears.

Spurred by their sorrows both of them became,
in their specific spheres, a famous name.
Mickey chose movies . . . and Herbert found
performing magic soothed his pains profound.

Is fate predetermined for any woman or man?
Do the divine forces dictate a plan?
Can fortunes change with love and hopes?
Does serendipity carve our horoscopes?

The Nivelli son, victim of religious outrage,
was of Mickey's disposition and his age.
When Mickey left my hospital . . . on his empty chair,
Peter appeared like an answer to my prayer."

Shifting Spirits

"Dear mother, my spirit in Mickey's body took root.
Mine was destroyed but I found a substitute . . .
with Mickey as a medium, I will be around you.
He will follow whatever I guide him to do."

The surrogate may not equal the quality
of the departed. Use of their physicality
in the interim, offers some relief.
The spirit is eternal – life is brief.
Ignorant and skeptical people call it a spoof.
Love for the believers is the only needed proof.

Skeptics even doubt God, yet when nearing death,
they exclaim, 'O God', before their last breath.
Divine echoes wane when the feelings aren't true.
In purity, love blossoms and chimes right on cue."

Hans shouted in anger, "This is not the way
intelligent people behave! I must have my say.
Our relationship with Mickey is a business deal.
This spiritual rubbish cannot be real."

Infusing Infinity

"Life's dreams or nightmares last only a while.
It is with the infinite that we must reconcile.
Eternity is our spiritual component's habitat.
Our fleeting life on earth must heed this fact.

Cynics will realize no one is really dead,
if spiritual consciousness is allowed to be bred.
The vistas of our being become infinitely greater
than existing perceptions, by trusting our Creator.

After people die on earth (I believe in this fact),
that they can live on, if their dreams are intact.
Dreams do not die in graves or a fire.
Love transcends every maze and mire.

Our spirits are not bound by worldly laws.
In his eternal form, Herbert last night was
whispering in my ears: 'Before you get older,
pursue the plan I want you to shoulder.'

I clearly heard Herbert's voice. Can this be done?
Felix and Herbert's voices sounding like one.
Through love's power I could hear them
like the exquisite rhymes of an ethereal poem.

'Time as you know, waits for no one.
Our mission is incomplete without a son.
If Hans is being difficult convince him somehow.'
Herbert left after tenderly kissing my brow.

Hans, this is my life's paramount mission.
Like a deathbed wish Herbert made this decision.
Nivelli, is a history, not just a name or a sound.
It is a challenge to people's prejudices profound.

With the tortures I suffered, my body was defiled.
So biologically I could not conceive a child.
Adoption can spiritually bestow a motherhood.
Hans retorted, 'Lotte, that is neither right nor good.
Lonely old people without children attract
those seeking to exploit them. This is a hard fact.'

Either you or I, one of us shall surely die
before the other, so it is imperative that we try
to make proper preparations for whoever is left behind.
Hans, we both are old and unwell. Who shall we find?

Human life's fleeting fun and mortal thrills
are inevitably followed by medicines and pills.
My mother's lonely death brings tears to my eyes.
Please compromise, Hans, before one of us dies."

Cosmic Connections

"One day Herbert's voice spoke. 'Please patiently wait . . .
for the unfolding events shall change your fate.'
My bonds with Mickey inexplicably grew.
Whenever I saw him Peter would slide into view.
It embarrassed Mickey when I'd gaze at his face.
It was Peter's features that I was trying to trace.

I was very sure that I had found Herbert's son.
My heart assured me that they both were one.
The hospital declared I could go . . . but, oh my,
I was strangely afraid to bid the place good-bye.

Mickey's visits there had soothed my pain.
If I returned home will he visit me again?
What bothered me was that once I return home,
Hans would curb Mickey's visits and I'd feel alone.

Whenever Hans was with me, I imagined Herbert there.
Hans would wonder at my expressions and blank stare.
With Herbert's smile and Peter's pictures on shelves,
my so many loves split me into several selves.

The ravage of religious radicals made millions die.
Millions of innocents suffered like Herbert and I.
Herbert was compelled to twist and reshape
his original name Lewin into Nivelli to escape
wicked religious distortions invoking the devil.
Personal agendas are cloaked by the medieval
dogmas of despots who exploit religious fears.
Hans reacted by narrating his pain of past years."

Hans Reveals his Hidden Horror

"Pets have no religion but the overzealous declared.
'All pets owned by Jews have got to be ensnared.'
We had a beloved pet, a dog named Lord.
My dog and I were victims of the Nazi maraud.

I had named him Lord, for he ruled my heart.
A faithful dog, very loving and smart.
His rapturous wagging soothed my strife.
He was the lord and the joy of my life.

With a fixed gaze, he would patiently await
my return home. Then he'd rush to the gate.
Barking lovingly and licking me with glee,
Lord pranced joyfully to welcome me.

With unbound love dogs are ready to sacrifice,
for their owners, their very own precious life.
Dog lovers know the pain of losing a dog.
Nazi abduction of Lord put my mind in a fog.

I asked them what they would do with him?
They replied with a wicked, vicious grin:
'Why should we tell you, if he lives or dies?
Your questions do not even merit our replies.'

They grabbed Lord's leash and began to pull.
Lord's struggle and resistance was very painful.
He dug in his paws. They dragged him all the way.
I heard him moan, 'Don't let them take me away.'

Lotte, Lord's farewell glances made me weep.
Did they give him food? Where did he sleep?
How harsh, I wondered, was their cruelty to him?
I was totally shattered from without and within.

Lord's pleading eyes haunt, as also his moans.
The pangs are sharper because of the unknowns.
Pains linger forever for a lost child or a pet.
Without proper closure, the victims never forget.

Lotte, I have learned to put *my* sorrows behind.
The memories that continue to haunt your mind,
must come to an end. Why continually lambaste
what can't be changed. Forget about the past!"

"Hans, your advice I know is well meant,
but to agree with you will not cure the ailment.
A healing starts when we begin learning
from failures and foibles. That's my yearning.

Human memory is often conditioned to dim
past painful cries that are dark and grim.
No one must ravage a mother's womb,
and send its fruits to an untimely tomb.

We have to expose every human crime.
Recalling can help to stir the sublime
layers of human memory which is short.
So Hans, I feel right in my need to exhort.

Criminals must not think they can behave
with impunity when they send innocents to a grave.
For all unknown victims I want to bear the cross.
Each life lost is an irreparable human loss."

A Biological Mother's Rights

"My commitment was so complete, I had begun
to deeply sense that Mickey was my spiritual son.
How will Amar Kaur, his biological mother, react
when she learns of her son's spiritual pact?

Mothers are known to be very possessive.
Strong maternal instincts make them defensive
about sharing their own children with another.
Protective and caring attributes define a 'mother'.

Herbert returned to goad me with his smile.
'Plead with Mickey's mother, she'll reconcile.'
His spirit always arrived when I needed to climb
any obstacle on my road and race against time.

He continued to magically bolster my intent.
I'd invite Mickey whenever Hans was absent.
What I learnt from him and whatever I knew
I'd narrate to Hans, to change his point-of-view."

Religious Divides

"Mickey was born in British-India where people enjoyed
a harmony between religions, which was destroyed
by politicians who exploited the bigoted and decided:
'Our God is different, so India must be divided!'

'Our religion is in danger!' was the call of bigotry,
deliberately designed to be inflammatory.
'God hates non-believers . . . we shall condemn
and destroy those belonging to another religion.'

With hate-filled sermons they ranted and raged.
Mob hysteria was ignited . . . an internal war waged.
The frenzy unleashed by exploiters of religions
was a political ploy that won them their legions.

'We are purest of the pure . . . we heard God speak.'
A belief eagerly embraced by the gullible and weak.
Religion was exploited for personal goals . . .
to achieve them, the sinners sold their souls.

Atrocities were inflicted and murders committed.
Indian against Indian was tragically pitted.
Religious conflagrations agonized heaven.
India was divided on August 15, 1947.

Self-serving leaders forced India to face
the splitting of families with painful disgrace.
England was forced to create in this world,
a new nation: Pakistan's flag was unfurled."

Diabolical Diversions

"Resources that could have uplifted the poor
were frittered in futile pursuits of war.
Money wasted on weapons could eradicate starvation.
Politicians had made false promises of salvation.

Indians had lived as one family for many centuries.
Doom and regression loom if they remain enemies.
Children of India – flowers of divine seeds
were divided by the exploiters of religions and creeds.

In God's garden we are flowers of humankind.
It is the divine duty of every leader to bind
flowers into bouquets, beautiful and upright,
for in each is reflected its Creator's light.

We are all gifted with a natural lifespan.
Can a religion ever sanction the killing of man?
True religion is only meant to bind
and not for the breakup of mankind.

No language contains enough words to describe
God's majesty and wonders. We can only subscribe
to His glory with constructive deeds. Songs or chants
have no meaning without the conduct God wants.

Empty words of praise are worthless and shoddy.
Honest work is worship if it helps somebody.
Praying and performing rituals all day long
is a waste of resources and blatantly wrong!
If words without deeds were God's sole need
then parrot-brained humans He would breed.

Indians targeted other Indians to be slaughtered.
Their wealth and women to the victors were offered
as trophies for having killed or mercilessly displaced
helpless civilians. Humanity was disgraced.

Pakistan or India, what's in a name?
The pain people suffer is all the same.
No religion encourages or condones sin.
Must politics smother the compassion within?

Divisive tactics that such villains use
are designed by the Devil to stoke abuse
of God's creations. Only people with inferior
dispositions need to project being 'superior'.

India's devastating division produced dubious gains
for the selfish politicians – but millions suffered pains.
India's potential was golden if it had remained united.
But diminished, when it was artificially divided."

Ravaging Religious Riots

"Through murder and mayhem Mickey's family strode
from Pakistan with paltry possessions for the road.
Ten-years-old Mickey began to wonder:
'Are we God's creations or His blunder?'

The victims were running, starving and suffering.
Some were trapped, others hopelessly cowering.
Fanatics believed their God would be more feared
if they flung babies up and have them speared.

The spilling of a single innocent child's blood,
shall sully any crusade, holy war or Jihad.
Does God create babies as objects for killing?
Did the perpetrators not have any sense or feeling?

Those who kill God's children cannot be sane.
They must be mad or with minds on the wane.
Hindus, Moslems, Christians, Sikhs or Jews
are all God's children . . . never objects for abuse."

Papa's Perils

"Love and responsibility provide people with strength.
Much can be endured but then at length,
with seven children to feed, Mickey's dad tried . . .
but Sujan Singh, his Papa, finally crumbled and died.

Mickey, still a child, bitterly began asking:
'Death, do you know the depth of your sting?
And fire, your macabre red dancing flame,
is forging for me a future full of pain.'

There was no edifice or monument that marked
the spot, where his cremated father had embarked
on his eternal journey. Seven children became fatherless.
This plunged the family into a very deep morass.

After the last rites all mourners dispersed.
Mickey later returned to the spot and burst
into a flood of tears that flowed unabated.
He lay in a heap where his father was cremated.

He embraced the earth and held a burnt ember.
'I'll miss you, Papaji, and forever remember,
that you were the victim of a distortion of Gods
and you lost the battle against uneven odds.'

The family was devastated, helpless and sore.
They were forced to leave their home in Jubbulpore
and migrate to Delhi on a mournful day.
This unknown future was a thousand miles away.

The only shelter offered by a relative
was part of a small house, the only alternative.
Seven siblings and a widow were all underfed.
Some slept on the floor for lack of a bed.

Hunger pangs began gnawing Mickey
and magnified his desperation hopelessly.
He found escape by watching movies.
It helped him cope with the harsh realities."

Lure of Show Business

"In the theatres or radio wherever he heard
songs from movies, his heart was stirred.
The surnames of many Indian movie stars,
were often changed to be called Kumars.

Ashok, Devanand, Dilip and Raj,
were names that loomed brilliant and large.
Mickey also wished that his surname be Kumar.
He hoped it would help him become a star.

He was a child, so these thoughts thrived.
With this troubled mindset he then strived
to be in India's Bollywood a thousand miles afar.
He ran away from home to avoid an uproar.

He had yet another problem that would greatly impair
his prospect . . . Sikh religion prohibited the cutting of hair.
Mickey's uncut hair would be an impediment . . .
in Bollywood, only men with short hair were relevant.

His religion's edict against cutting of hair or shaving
was imposed long ago when battles were raging.
Long hair and turbans served to shield the head.
These rules, in that setting, were wisely bred."

Sacred Symbols

"The five religious symbols, the great Sikh Guru chose,
in those times, were a boon for Sikhs against foes.
A comb; long hair; steel bracelet; under-garment and sword –
were the required accessories for a ready-to-combat squad.

Great leaders of yore were very inventive.
In present times too they would be innovative.
They would reform the edicts that had lost their worth.
Why perpetuate traditions that impede human growth?

It is the mindless fanatics who fan extreme notions.
Often solely to serve their personal promotions.
A few Sikhs rebelled and could dare
to yield to the needs of cutting their hair.

Orthodox parents who felt that this defiled
the religion, punished or disowned the rebel child.
In India's Bollywood, long hair was considered strange.
To pursue his prospects, Mickey was forced to change.

It is prudent for all progressive religions to afford
an open-minded dialogue and a viable accord.
Times and tides change – compromises are inevitable.
Pragmatic rules make religious obligations tenable.

Ancient teachings, adages and superstitions,
are justifiably superseded by our spiritual missions.
Does a soul have a religion, class or creed?
Man-made divisions make humanity bleed.

It is counter-productive for a minority,
to brandish differences to the majority.
By cultivating noble intents and an open mind
goodwill is propelled and differences left behind.

The best religious teachings are those that begin
molding a child's psyche with love and discipline.
The worst are teachings that condemn fellow humans
for all of us are God's beloved daughters and sons.

For God it is substance, and not ceremony, that matters.
He disapproves of cobwebbed norms and fetters.
Mickey reposed his faith in his inner guidelines.
He decided to adapt with the changing times.

Visions beyond symbols helped Mickey to brave
the wrath of his family. He decided to shave
the outward displays. His maverick mind began
reasoning that rituals alone do not make a man.

Would the great Guru of Sikhs be angry or sad
if this obsolete rule was discarded by this lad?
To be damned for cutting hair seems rather odd!
Can such extreme reactions be expected of God?

The Creator is more charitable to His creations
than human beings with narrow-minded interpretations.
To outdated edicts, Mickey's ears were shut.
He had a valid reason for having to cut
his hair despite the price. This he understood
would hurt initially – but then turn into good."

Rebel with a Cause

"Mickey was fourteen-years-old when he found
that his values and decisions were quite sound.
The primary purpose of a soul's physical birth
is to avail of opportunities that uplift its worth.

Though Delhi was also a humming center
of barbershops, Mickey was afraid to enter . . .
in case someone who knew him could walk in
and stop the act by branding it a 'sin'.

As a precaution, he boarded a train
and traveled to Agra to remain
incognito, then with utmost care,
found a secluded barber to cut his hair.

His trepidation made him check every side
before he had the courage to zip inside.
The barber's seat felt like an electric chair.
It shot charged emotions through the air
making Mickey burst into a flood of tears.
He had never cut his hair in fourteen years.

Mickey's crying upset everyone in the shop.
The barber was alarmed and wanted to stop.
Mickey delved deep into his heroic soul.
He wiped his tears to regain self-control.
He paid the barber his fee and hastily left.
For the first time in life, of long hair bereft.

Without religious symbols he felt rather strange.
Pain and promise mingled with this change.
Mickey, who was Harbhajan Singh, now became
Harbance Kumar – he assumed a fresh new name."

Mickey, photographed in Delhi at the tender age of 13, is wearing the traditional turban, which covered his long uncut hair.

Peter Nivelli.

Lotte would often study Peter and Mickey's photographs for similarities in their features.

India's Bollywood

"Mickey traveled to Bollywood as Harbance Kumar.
This new name, he hoped, would make him a star.
He was one of the many thousand aspiring others,
who arrive with high hopes, but nobody bothers.

Each one with hopes to carve a name . . .
claim their glory and bask in fame.
Soon when hunger pangs began to gnaw,
no one was a friend when the pains were raw.

Mickey slept on streets and tirelessly tread
in search of a job to buy some bread.
Nothing was offered, though he tried and tried.
At last he wrote home, swallowing his pride.

He asked his family if they could help him.
Because he cut his hair their reaction was grim.
He was rejected, dismissed, scorned and taunted.
'We wish you were dead – you are unwanted.'

When he received their letter, he bitterly wept.
Hungry and all alone on alley streets he slept.
Rejection by his family made him feel outworn.
He felt very lonely, abandoned and forlorn."

Blood Money

"One day, by a hospital that was top-notch,
he saw a sad plight and began to watch
the feeble and the hungry, who patiently stood,
before a blood bank to sell their blood for food.

Feeling like them, he joined the band.
To sell his blood, he began to stand
amidst the needy, his heart turned to steel.
The money only bought a few days meal.

With a heavy heart and a few coins so precious,
he gazed at luckier children and was envious.
Some played cricket, others went to college.
He wished he could afford the pursuit of knowledge.

A stable childhood and love are very crucial.
For the formative years, this is greatly essential.
Mickey's job hunting was desperate and sad.
Every film studio's gate would shut on this lad.

Relentlessly he walked from street to street
with tattered clothes and blistered feet.
He did not falter but continued to seek
work without food and chances so bleak.

Challenges can strengthen powers of the will.
The coddled may not develop such a survival skill.
With persistent pursuits, he got a film extra's part.
That modest start helped to console his heart."

Payoff for Persistence

"Filmistan Studio's manager, S.L. Puri, noted
that Mickey was humble and very devoted.
He told him sincerely, 'I like your pluck.
Your positive attributes have changed your luck.
People can be qualified but lack sincerity.
Or work with diminished passion and ability.
They cannot match your drive or persistence.
I like your fire, I will hire your assistance.'

Mickey worked very hard. He did not ramble,
smoke cigarettes, do drugs, drink or gamble.
To compensate for his incomplete education
he'd work harder with greater determination.

While others indulged in fun and frolic,
he furthered his future by being a workaholic.
Education from life's hard-knock schools,
often provides better skills and tools.

Most useful of these virtues is the one of frugality.
Moderation and a simple life enhance your capability.
Success goes where midnight lamps burn bright.
To hard working people luck extends its light.

Towards the deserving, right opportunities gravitate.
Who with laggards would want to associate?
Mickey worked to optimize his inner resources.
If God's gifts are cherished, He too rejoices."

The West-Indian Chapter

Hans belittled these achievements: "Mickey is guilty
of abandoning projects. Don't you see it, Lotte?
He is here after dumping his other operations . . .
how can you trust him with your redemptions?"

"Before passing judgment Hans, hear all I say.
About 100 years ago Indians were shipped away
by their British rulers. To the West Indies they arrived
as indentured labor and of their motherland deprived.

When this migration started, their forefathers were young
so the current generation hardly knows their mother tongue.
They learned what the master's spoke, but their immense
love for India continued. Old bonds remained intense.

There is hardly an Indian in the West Indies,
who does not yearn or dream to cross the seas
to visit India. It's in their blood and every breath!
They wish to feel India's heartbeat before their death.

They were taken on ancient ships. Thus, it seemed
travel back was impossible. Yet, they dreamed
of their roots. They cultivated every link and idea
to remain connected with the traditions of India.

Indian cultural imports built bridges in their heart.
They saw Indian movies for their music and art.
Today about a million Indian West-Indians
are Guyanese, Surinamese or Trinidadians.

Indian movies for them had become a rage.
Their demand had increased . . . reaching the stage
of cinemas clamoring to screen them each day.
Mickey arrived in the West Indies for this foray.

He succeeded so well that soon he had
to shift his headquarters to Trinidad.
In the exotic West Indies Mickey soon became
an innovative showman and earned a big name.

He met Mahadeo Ramdial who toiled without stop
in a transport business. Ramdial was a top
sugarcane contractor who reached his position,
from poverty, by sheer hard work and dedication.

An industrious disposition and opportunity are luck's
required ingredients. Ramdial acquired a fleet of trucks.
When his success spiraled, it aroused the jealousy
of his peers who squandered their resources in revelry.

"The 'India-born' tag, coupled with Mickey's vigor,
made him eligible as did his handsome figure." – Lotte

Mahadeo Ramdial and his wife Rookmin saw,
in this man from India, a future son-in-law.
Some West-Indian families find a greater joy
in marrying their daughters to an Indian boy.

The 'India-born' tag, coupled with Mickey's vigor,
made him eligible as did his handsome figure.
Diligent desires become a reality. To their joy and pride,
their daughter – Chand Ramdial – became Mickey's bride.

Then Mickey began sponsoring from his motherland,
dancers and singers. Vyjayanthimala, I understand
was a top star . . . so you can easily guess
that her show he imported was a great success."

Mickey fulfils another fond dream. Seen at the world famous symbol of eternal love, Taj Mahal, from left to right: Mickey and his wife, Chand, adopted son Navin, in-laws Rookmin Ramdial and Mahadeo Ramdial.

Pioneering a Film Industry

"The first ever West-Indian movie Mickey began to shoot.
'A movie pioneer of the West Indies' became his repute.
For no one before had done this in Trinidad.
No guts, no glory, was the motto of this lad.

He had to start from scratch, so he placed an order
for new movie cameras, lights and sound recorder.
His movie *The Right and The Wrong*, in a Film Festival
was acclaimed for its theme and it won a gold medal."

"Mickey is smart," Hans condescended, "But do
please remember, Lotte, that he is *not* a Jew.
To me frankly, he is a cad. This is what I really fear.
He left India, went to West Indies . . . now he's here."

"Hans, instability rocked the region so Mickey migrated.
The political and other upheavals suddenly suffocated
his business ventures. He produced and directed
Girl from India in America, which was well-accepted."

Men who are Cads

"Hans, consider this selfless task he undertook.
This I hope will make you change your outlook.
In matters of parenting some men are bad.
A father who abandons children is the real cad.

Two brothers-in-law of Mickey had been gifted
with God's five children, whose fathers then drifted.
By the plight of four fatherless daughters and one son
both Mickey and Chand's hearts were overcome.

Men may err but the man who is a deserter,
of God's helpless creations, is a cad and a traitor.
Chand and Mickey's sisters now had to redeem
their children's welfare from a shattered dream.

Mickey showered them fatherly love and guidance.
Chand said, 'My motherhood must remain in abeyance.
Let these five needy children, though not from my body,
be linked to my heart in a divine rhapsody.

Their fragile feelings have been deeply hurt.
They could feel insecure if I too gave birth
to biological children. I can satisfy my need
through them. If I hurt them – my heart shall bleed.
None of God's creations must ever be abandoned.
Biological or adopted, by all children I am enchanted.

Behind every innocent face reflects God's very own.
Parenting is not merely seeds being sown.
Biotechnology too makes babies, but the nephew and nieces
that God has placed in our care, are divine masterpieces.'

Blessed are those with such a magnificent magnitude.
Emotional bonds are greater than biological parenthood.
Chand gave her best to the five very equally.
God sees all so she'll be rewarded celestially.
Each deserting parent is a sinner and coward.
Whose soul shall suffer? Who will divinity reward?

Parents neglecting children, who God decides
to be placed in their care, hurt precious lives!
The 'Eternal Watcher' sees all so no lies or lame
excuses shall mitigate a deserter's sin and shame.

By absconding from responsibility they jeopardize
a helpless child's welfare. Divinity does despise
this sin very much for it effectively replaces
their innocent smiles with sorrowful faces.

When children grow up their needs increase.
Mickey provided for his nephew and each niece.
Some even called him 'Papa,' as a way of addressing.
God always compensates people with His blessing.

Each girl, into an angelic achiever can blossom.
Endeavors of boys help to make them handsome.
Chand and Mickey were amply challenged.
The fathers who fled, their souls were damaged."

Prisoner of Dogmas

Hans had a closed mind so he was not impressed.
Xenophobia is a condition not easily redressed.
"Because Mickey is not Jewish I reject your plea."
Enlightenment alone could set Hans free.

Mindsets forged by religion are like hardened cement.
Doctrines instilled since childhood are not easily bent.
"Lotte, I will help you in your mission,
only if you follow our Jewish tradition.
Mickey is from India. He must not be chosen!
Your obstinate decision I find very brazen.
Take my advice Lotte, and banish the thought.
Your rebellion against tradition is wrongly wrought.
The spiritual banter that you profusely expound
has impaired your judgment – it is not sound.
Never ever adopt someone who is not our kind.
Your wading in afterlife has made you blind."

"To get compassion from Hans I was so frantic.
A woman's despair can turn psychosomatic.
If only men understood feminine pangs,
they'd empathize instead of baring their fangs.

Hans, this fulfillment shall herald my victory.
My defeat of the radicals shall be humanity's glory.
A surge of spiritual energies tells me that I should
transcend banal barriers to attain motherhood.

Herbert is goading me from God's blue immensity.
My mission now assumes a greater intensity.
Tragedies like Peter's must not be repeated.
The misguided fanatics must be defeated.

My spiritual son's saga may help to spotlight
what children suffer when the grown-ups fight.
Peter's story may inspire, as it must indeed,
the need for tolerance by every class and creed.
Hans your attitude is conflicting and contrary,
to the values I espouse and the name *Nivelli.*"

"Lotte, I insist that you reverse your decision.
Your spooky spirituality deserves my derision.
Going along with you shall make me an abettor
of misguided choices. Find a Jewish successor."

Subversion of Reason

"Hans, the use of God or religion to inflame
prejudice between people is a sin and shame.
Godliness is reflected in faiths that include
compassionate teachings to promote brotherhood.

You are a good man, Hans, but sadly I find,
that racial prejudice has closed your mind.
Religious considerations foist a narrow limit.
I apply vaster visions to examine Mickey's merit.
Closed human minds regress and lose power.
If I let that happen my growth will not flower.

The chalice of every fanatic is a poison cup.
Manipulators brew it and the mindless drink it up.
The drinkers become zombies – without any hope.
Like blind sheep or cattle sliding on a steep slope.

Any religious reason for raping or plunder
is a sin that tears the human fabric asunder.
For our spiritual son, Peter, who was burnt alive,
my commitment to his soul must and shall survive.

Ostriches and cowards hide in the sand from truth.
Violation of human rights anywhere is uncouth.
Injustice anywhere spreads to be a threat
to everyone, everywhere – we must not forget."

Destiny's Detours

"New technologies crushed movie business in their grip.
VCR's and DVD's forced Mickey into salesmanship
of real estate in New York. He had to adapt and plod.
Were these bad times or subtle nudges of God?

Shall Mickey's biological mother deny me the smile
that had brightened my life and days all this while?
Will God grant me the courage to plead and ask
his mother for her son – a very daunting task.

Like dried earth, my maternity that was cracked
could not get the glory that I had yearned and lacked.
Amar Kaur, Mickey's mother, could gift the element
that would fulfill Herbert's dream. Would she relent?"

Amar Kaur was orphaned when she was barely ten years old. Later, she became a widow at the age of 40. Without a home or income, she brought up and educated her seven children by pawning and selling her wedding jewels. Her children were pivotal to her life. Could she willingly share one of her sons with Lotte Nivelli?

Lotte Pleads

"God has graced you with seven children.
Of your seven, I only ask you for one.
Nowhere did I find, however hard I'd trace,
the right person to occupy my Peter's place.

I must have a son for our mission to complete.
Please have pity on my needs and tired feet.
I do have a tacit approval from heaven.
Peter and Mickey were both born in 1937.

Mickey complements Peter and is of his age.
With your gift, my book will find its final page.
For years I had searched every cranny and nook.
No one is more qualified to complete my book.

With Mickey my dreams can be fulfilled at last.
Many people shall benefit from our past.
Amar Kaur was magnanimous and she consented.
My next need then to Mickey, I presented . . . "

Sacrificing Past Glory

"Mickey, I need you to change your famous name.
It was Herbert's wish that Nivelli be your surname.
Your fame in India and West Indies is the price
which my mission needs you to please sacrifice.

Mickey agreed . . . to wipe the Nivelli tears.
The Nivelli name would revive after so many years.
It was Herbert's dream that his name remain alive.
He had twirled Lewin to Nivelli just to survive.

Mickey sacrificed the laurels of his 'Kumar' name
by legally adopting Nivelli as his surname.
This gave him the right to be my spiritual son.
Peter's reincarnation had earnestly begun.

Then came the moment I did patiently crave.
I took Mickey to meet Herbert at his grave.
His mortal remains are here without his essence
but I can feel his fulfilled spiritual presence.

Mickey folded his hands and knelt at the grave.
A surge of emotions heaved like a wave.
I could see Herbert smile which helped me stop
the flow of tears that were aching to drop.

Under the witness of both the moon and sun,
I exclaimed, 'Herbert, behold your son!
By my relentless search of so many years,
I have found the one who will wipe my tears.
He mirrors your virtues and your stalwart build.
My promise to you is complete and fulfilled.'

Upon reaching my goal after all these years,
I could not stem the swelling flood of tears.
The agonies of my life seemed to wash away.
Hope had arrived on silver wings to stay.
A mother and son, who fate had put together,
both began weeping and they embraced each other.

A mother's tears and a father's grave
were the final formalities needed to pave
my pathway to motherhood. I had to re-adjust.
In my newfound son I reposed all my trust."

Like millions, who are blinded by religion's fervor, Hans remained adamant. He shut his ears to Lotte's pleas for spiritualism, love and understanding.

The Standoff

"Why did you do it? Did he mislead you?
Lotte, I insist Mickey must not succeed you!
If you die before me, I will undo your mistake.
I shall *have* to fight if only for our religion's sake."

"Hans, it's high time we end this taboo.
We all must remember that Jesus was a Jew.
The divisions created by caste and creed
are poisons that make humanity bleed.

As Jews we have suffered, so I never will . . .
let these dreadful distinctions prevent me to fulfill
the dreams of Herbert. This is my decision.
Hans, your narrow outlook needs a revision.

Such attitudes launched the holocaust . . .
why must more innocents be killed or lost?
Bigotry and narrow norms are the premises
that cause upheavals and civilization's nemesis.
The dividing walls must collapse along with the hate.
Beyond our bodies, all distinctions evaporate.

Our souls learn lessons from this life's spectrums
to ascend to the echelons of becoming humans.
By promoting goodness and humane sensitivity
we earn accolades that brighten our eternity.

Nirvana or Salvation – whatever be the name –
at the end of the road our goal is the same.
Willful sins inevitably spiral a regression . . .
while virtues propel our soul's progression."

The Miracle

Lotte awoke from her coma. She surprised us and said,
"You must not be sad or mourn when I am dead.
My body is a vessel that is merely being shed
so that I may don eternal apparels instead.

With evolution's grand design my soul shall soar
to the progressive opening of my next door.
Mickey, please remember Hans was with me
for over twenty years. He will be lonely . . .

So after I have gone, Mickey, I plead
that you must fulfill Hans' every need.
He is rather old, so I sincerely pray
that you be by his side every day.

For my sake, please treat him like a King.
From my new home I'll be watching everything."
I made my commitment to her most faithfully
and vowed to fulfill the promise diligently.

During the final phase of her life, Lotte was dependant upon Mickey and the wheelchair for mobility. Here they are seen visiting the Taj Mahal, an Indian emperor's monument to undying love.

"Hans, regarding Mickey, please respect my decision.
He is our mission's veritable redemption . . .
Mickey and Peter's entities are now one.
Herbert and I finally found our son.
I must bid good-bye for I see an array
of my loved ones arriving from far away . . .
for our long-awaited heavenly reunion.
We'll never be separated in this dominion.
Our love made us worthy of this eternal home
but I will keep in touch for my spirit can roam."

Loving souls beyond the range of mortal sight
began preparing Lotte for her celestial flight.
For an eternal reunion they were taking her away
from her disposable abode of human clay.

I cradled her until her very last breath.
She smiled serenely before embracing death.
The birds stopped singing in the trees.
I folded my hands and fell on my knees.

Hans survived Lotte for almost 5 years and was confined to a wheelchair during his last days. Mickey willingly heeded Lotte's deathbed request to look after the daily welfare of her companion, Hans, because it would soothe her soul. Each day, as they traveled through many countries, Mickey could see Lotte's contented smile transmitted from the Heavens above.

The Transformation

Hans changed dramatically after that day.
Lotte's light, he said, illumined his pathway.
He heard her echoes and began to jolt.
The epiphany hit him like a thunderbolt.

His lips quivered, he trembled and cried:
"Lotte's spirit is alive . . . she never died.
Mickey, I am wiser. I had been misled . . .
I realize now, that no one is ever dead.

I clearly hear from the heavens above
Lotte's ethereal echoes of eternal love.
At last I found my spiritual anchor
when Lotte narrated this astral encounter:

'In heaven, Felix and I went for a walk,
there we met a dog who began to talk.'
'I am Lord,' he said. 'Hans' dog on earth.
When they killed me, I got heavenly birth.
In heaven, Lotte, as your now realize –
we animals can talk and are also wise.'

'For your dog, Hans, both Felix and I feel
a very special love. We often share a meal.
Lord told us his love for you and his bond
is much stronger. Love thrives beyond.

He misses you very much and anxiously awaits
your arrival here. He'll rush to heaven's gates
when your term on earth is over and done.
Lord shall be the first to greet you 'Welcome.'

He has arranged for a party and a dance
along with his friends to welcome you, Hans.
His friends are a cat, goat, lion and parakeet.
They are always together to play, sleep or eat.

In heaven, lions lovingly loll with goats.
Here no one grabs each other's throats.
Pure love prevails and is paramount
for it is sustained by The Divine Fount.'"

Enlightenment

Do you want a recipe for relief?
It is possible through Lotte's belief
that ultimately it is only the power of love
that prevails to reward you in heavens above.
It has greater worth than all this world's gold.
The dynamics of love dwell in your heart's fold.

So shun the thoughts that cause strife
and accentuate love to enrich afterlife.
Defeat this life's adversities by the sublime
love like Lotte's . . . it transcends space and time!
You too can realize humanity's final frontiers
by tuning in to hear these celestial whispers:

*"From fears and pains a perpetual release
awaits you in My Habitat of Eternal Peace.
What you did on earth to cultivate love,
shall echo eternally in the heavens above."*